The
POTTER'S
Project Book

Burnished pots by Peter Cosentino

Non-functional pieces of work still have links with the
techniques involved in work of a more practical nature.
These composite pots were speckled with different colour
slips and burnished before firing.

The POTTER'S
Project Book

PETER COSENTINO

CHARTWELL
BOOKS, INC.

Published in North America by
Chartwell Books Inc.,
A Division of Book Sales Inc.,
110, Enterprise Avenue,
Secaucus
New Jersey 07094

First impression 1987
Copyright © 1987 The Paul Press Limited
All rights reserved.

ISBN 1-5521-150-X

Typeset by AKM Associates (U.K.) Ltd.,
Ajmal House, Hayes Road, Southall, London UB2 5NG
Origination by South Sea International, Hong Kong
Printed in the UK through
Print Buyer's Database Ltd

This book was edited, designed and produced by
The Paul Press Ltd., 22, Bruton Street, London W1X 7DA

Art Editor	Antony Johnson
Project Editor	Emma Warlow
Editorial	Vicky Waters
Photography	David Sheppard
Line illustrations	Hayward & Martin Ltd., Ian Bott
Index	Kathy Gill

Art Director	Stephen McCurdy
Managing Editor	Elizabeth Longley
Editorial Director	Jeremy Harwood
Publishing Director	Nigel Perryman

Contents

Foreword

This book is dedicated to my wife Mandy, and to Thomas and Matthew, my two sons. I would like to thank Emma, Antony and Vicky from The Paul Press for helping to make working on this book such a happy experience, and my special thanks must go to David Sheppard, the photographer whose sensitive work has contributed so much to the projects.

Anyone who has watched an experienced thrower at work cannot fail to be amazed by the almost magical ease with which the successive vessels seem to flow from his fingers. In reality, of course, a potter's confidence and masterful skill stem from years of patient practice and determined hard work. It would be foolish to suggest that a beginner can achieve the same results; nevertheless, competent throwing is well within the reach of anyone who is prepared to put effort into learning the basic skills and techniques. Many students surprise themselves with the quality of their first efforts.

In this book, I have tried to plan projects of varying complexity, so that both the beginner and the more advanced potter can enjoy making all sorts of attractive and functional pieces of pottery that stretch their personal ability. It is also designed to provide busy pottery teachers with a solution when their pupils have grasped the basics of throwing and need a range of new challenges to keep them occupied.

There are never enough pages in any book to cover all the information that the author wants to convey. **The Potter's Project Book** is no exception. Although I would be the first to acknowledge the importance of considering the complete design process from the first stages of planning, through construction and decoration, to glazing and firing, the true concern of this book is the actual business of throwing. I have therefore explained the decorative technique of using textured rollers to imprint the clay, because it is undertaken during throwing rather than when the form has dried. Like all the suggested decoration, this technique can be used on any of the projects in the book. The other techniques and the types of glaze that should be used to create the specific effects illustrated are briefly outlined at the end of each project. All these projects have been fired to a temperature of 1250°C in an electric kiln.

There is never any one correct way to make a particular item. No matter what the basic criteria are that determine the basic styling of any functional piece of pottery, (such as ease of handling, steadiness and durability), they can all be fulfilled in completely different ways. Two casseroles, for instance, can have differing lid fittings and handles and be made from very different clays, yet they will both be just as efficient. Throughout the book, I have tried to emphasize that my way is not necessarily the best, and is certainly not the only, way to make any of the projects I have covered. The techniques I employed were those that I find the easiest, and are therefore recommended as a starting point for the development of your own personal style and technique — which is after all the central aim of the book. The development of an indvidual style can only progress from the gradual exploration of personal ideas and technique. With this in mind, **The Potter's Project Book** has been designed to stimulate creativity and to provide the reader with a sound guide on which to base his experimentation.

Pottery making in any shape or form should always be enjoyable. I hope that *you* find making all of the projects fun and that your appetite is wetted to explore this fascinating activity further. It has besotted me for the past twenty years and thankfully shows no sign of letting up.

Happy potting!

The Principles
of Throwing

Creating beautiful thrown pottery at the wheel with
the confidence of a professional potter should be
within the reach of most pottery enthusiasts.
Throwing relies not only on skill and experience, but
on a thorough understanding of the different clays,
wheel types, tools and techniques. Truly expert
throwing can only be achieved once the essential
factors that have shaped the technique are
understood. I have always considered throwing to be
the most exciting of all pottery techniques, largely by
virtue of the demands it places on the potter and the
sense of personal achievement that comes
with success.

Clay manufacture and preparation

Although it is impossible to pinpoint the exact time at which the potter's wheel came into use, or indeed name its inventor, it is nevertheless generally accepted that by 2000 BC the wheel was being used widely and that it originated in Egypt. Prior to its introduction, functional pottery vessels were made using hand forming techniques, coiling being one of the most popular. It is easy to imagine how a potter creating a coil pot might have placed his clay on a surface which could be rotated to facilitate building the walls of the form. This could well have instigated the use of the wheel for throwing.

The invention of the wheel as a means of producing pottery enabled potters to increase their output dramatically. Throwing also promoted a fresh look at the possibilities of pottery design and a new subtlety of form emerged. Decorative devices based on drawing horizontal lines on to the revolving form became a recognizable feature of wheelthrown pottery and marked a move away from the more utilitarian ware of the past.

Refinements in the actual technique of throwing and improvements in wheel technology have advanced considerably over the years, but basic throwing techniques and the essential principle of the wheel have altered relatively little. In some countries today, primitive wheels are in everyday use and although they often comprise of little more than a heavy disc mounted on a fulcrum, rotated by hand or by foot, the craftsmanship of the vessels produced is quite remarkable. Although nowadays industrial manufacturing processes rely on jiggers and jolleys, casting and extrusion for their mass production, the wheel still seems to be as popular as ever. It enables the potter to make a wide variety of different forms relatively quickly compared to other hand forming pottery processes, and it never compromises individual creativity.

Throwing
Throwing is the process by which a wheelhead with variable rotational speeds is used to assist the hand forming of a homogeneous mass of soft plastic clay. Successful throwing is well within the reach of most people, but in common with all pottery techniques, success is not merely dependent on expertise. A good technique alone will not necessarily succeed if it is not put to use in conjunction with the correct type of clay. Throwing demands more from clay than any other pottery technique, because the clay must be suited to quick forming on the wheel; it must be sensitive enough to permit easy shaping; and at the same time it has to be rigid enough to ensure that the thrown form retains its shape while it is still wet.

Suitable throwing clays
Naturally occurring clays are numerous and vary enormously in appearance, chemical composition and in their behaviour during forming and firing. Nevertheless, all natural clays are classified into two categories: Primary and Secondary clays. This classification is based on whether the clay has been dug at its site of origin, when it is termed Primary, or whether it has since been transported to some other site by weathering elements and is therefore termed Secondary.

The purest clays are the primary clays, sometimes known as "residual". Not only does the action of the elements on the parent granite rock over the centuries serve to decompose the rock into clay, but also to transport the clay to other sites, often hundreds of miles away. China clay, or Kaolin, is the commonest form of primary clay. Deposits are found in and around granite outcrops.

Secondary clays are the most common of naturally occurring clays. Although these clays, like primary clays, originate from feldspathic rock, the transportation of the clay by rivers or glaciers and the effects of weathering alter the two most important characteristics of the clay. The particle size of secondary clay, which determines the "plasticity", or the suitability of a clay for use in pottery work, differentiates it from primary clay, as does the "contamination" by the variety of impurities it collects during its transportation.

Secondary differences
The size of the particles in secondary clay are smaller than those in primary clay, with the result that secondary clays are far more plastic. As the clay is transported from its site of origin, the particles are ground down. Running water is largely responsible for this grinding process, and it also sorts the particles into grades of fineness in a process known as "levigation". When particles of different sizes are carried along in flowing water, the larger, heavier particles settle first, leaving the finer grains suspended. It is usual, therefore, to find clays with a large particle formation on mature river beds, while those with fine particle formation are found some distance away, often deposited in lagoons or lakes. These clays are often referred to as being "sedimentary".

The impurities most commonly found in secondary clays are carbon material and iron oxide. Although carbon material within a clay may well affect its natural colour and assist plasticity, it burns away during the first firing. In some cases, a dark coloured clay will fire to a white or off-white colour. Iron oxide unless removed by special magnetic processes, remains in the clay throughout and affects the clay in terms of both its final fired colour, (clays with considerable iron content fire from a light tan to dark brown), and the maximum temperature it can withstand when fired. Iron oxide acts as a powerful flux in clays and as a result, many locally found clays with a high iron content cannot be fired to temperatures in excess of 1000 degrees. If they are, they begin to fuse and actually melt in a process called "vitrification" and the clay turns into a glass-like substance.

Preparation of secondary clays

The most common examples of secondary clay are ball clays, fireclays, and "brick clays" or marls. Naturally occurring clay is rarely in the right condition for throwing without further additions or blending. Most potters add to or alter secondary clay until they develop a clay that they can guarantee will behave in particular ways. Once a clay is treated to alter its natural characteristics, it is known as a "body". Although many experienced potters will prefer to develop specific clays themselves, specifically suited to their own needs, there is nothing to prevent potters with limited time or experience purchasing a manufactured ready-prepared body. I have used Potterycrafts "Throwers' Stoneware" clay for the projects in this book.

Apart from the mixing and blending of particular clays to obtain a body for successful throwing, fine sands and a material called "grog" are also added to improve the body's handling and firing characteristics. Grog is in fact clay that has been biscuit fired and then ground down to a particular grade of coarseness. The addition of sand or grog is usually undertaken to compensate for too much plasticity in a clay. Such clays are referred to as "fat" clays. If the clay is not plastic enough, it is termed "lean" or "short", and ball clay, which is highly plastic, is often added to remedy this deficiency.

The addition of sands and grog improves the working quality of over-plastic clay, increases its strength and gives it an open texture. This open texture allows the clay to dry more evenly, thus reducing the risk of warping or cracking. This process is known as giving the clay "bite" or "tooth". Because it has already been fired, the presence of grog within a clay also helps to minimize the shrinkage that occurs during firing when the water content of the clay is lost. The addition of grog also enables a clay to withstand highet temperatures. If a clay is not plastic enough, ball clay, which is highly plastic, can be added.

The clay manufacturing process

A raw clay is dug or mined and then crushed before being reduced to a liquid state called a "slip". A "blunger" is used to make slip. This machine works like a domestic food mixer, with a rotating blade in a tank breaking down the clay and mixing it with water until it becomes liquid. Blunged slip is then passed through special sieving screens which trap any unwanted materials such as grit and coarse sands. When a white body is required, slip can be passed across electro magnets which eliminate the iron content that would otherwise colour the clay.

The slip is then fed into a machine comprising of a series of large cloth bags. This is called a filter press. The water is squeezed out of the clay in this machine as the full bags of slip are mechanically pressed. The resulting cakes or slabs of clay are either allowed to dry, to be crushed at a later date and packaged as powdered clay or used as an additive in other clays, or they are kept in their plastic state and passed through a "pugmill". A pugmill is a long metal tube comprising a feed section, or "hopper", at one end, a middle section containing a powerful mixing blade, and a tapered end section that forces the clay to be compressed as it is extruded. The compression of the clay forces much of the air trapped within the clay to be expelled, but there are industrial pugmills available, called "de-airing" pugmills, which ensure that any air is completely removed.

Powdered or plastic clay?

Experienced studio potters usually develop their own personal body mixture so that they can guarantee that the clay they throw will behave in specific ways. It is obviously desirable to experiment with small amounts of raw materials when developing a new body and it is quite possible to mix powdered clays into a plastic consistency in much the same way as you would mix cement — on a clean floor using a shovel to turn the mixture and adding water to it gradually. Although time-consuming, mixing bodies from powder allows you to produce accurate clay combinations. It is also far more economical to buy clays in powder form.

The disadvantages of purchasing clays in powdered form are self-evident. For the beginner, or even the experienced potter who prefers the making process to preparation, being able to buy a plastic clay that needs relatively little further preparation prior to use can be cost effective. Consequently, most potters buy prepared clay in a plastic "ready-to-use" state, packed in 25kg (55lbs) blocks. Sand, grog, and other types of plastic clay can all be mixed into the clay, as described on p11.

Which clay to purchase

Although this book is concerned with throwing, it is important to consider various other important aspects of pottery before you choose your clay. Arguably, the most important of these is deciding to which temperature your work will need to be fired. Although a clay classified as stoneware (which can be fired to 1250–1300°C) can usually be fired at the lower temperature (900–1200°C) suited to earthenware, the reverse is not true. Some clays, particularly "red" clays cannot normally be fired at temperatures in excess of 1150°C without the risk of considerable warpage, bloating, or even melting.

Your choice of clay should also be determined by the final colour and texture you require. Your personal taste will obviously affect the type of pottery you want to produce, but factors such as the type of firing the clay is to receive should also be kept in mind when you choose your basic materials. The texture and colour of a piece of pottery will depend on whether it receives reduction or oxidised firing, and not just on the combination of clays in the body.

It is crucial to bear these considerations in mind when you are trying to choose the best clay for the type of work you plan to undertake. It is advisable to opt for a good general purpose throwing clay, at least to begin with. Look in manufacturers' catalogues for a clay suited to your needs – you may need one that is suited to throwing *and* hand forming for example. If you have attended pottery classes, find out from your tutor which clay you have been using and use this information as a guide when you come to buy your own. Most manufacturers sell their clays in small quantities as well as in bulk and, although expensive, small samples are ideal for experimenting with to discover which is the right clay body for your needs.

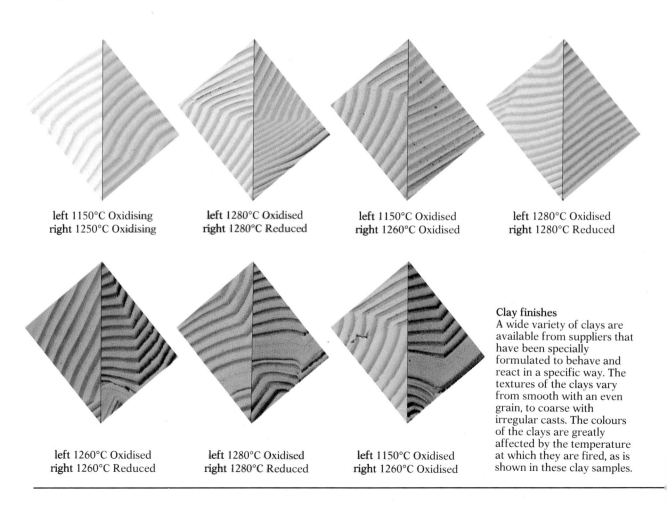

left 1150°C Oxidising
right 1250°C Oxidising

left 1280°C Oxidised
right 1280°C Reduced

left 1150°C Oxidised
right 1260°C Oxidised

left 1280°C Oxidised
right 1280°C Reduced

left 1260°C Oxidised
right 1260°C Reduced

left 1280°C Oxidised
right 1280°C Reduced

left 1150°C Oxidised
right 1260°C Oxidised

Clay finishes

A wide variety of clays are available from suppliers that have been specially formulated to behave and react in a specific way. The textures of the clays vary from smooth with an even grain, to coarse with irregular casts. The colours of the clays are greatly affected by the temperature at which they are fired, as is shown in these clay samples.

Clay preparation

Good throwing requires more than merely finding a good throwing clay and developing a successful throwing technique. The clay has to be in good working condition, or "well-prepared", before you can think about beginning to throw, since throwing demands a high quality clay.

A well-prepared clay should be of an even, soft consistency, have an evenly distributed water content and be free of any air pockets. Although bought plastic clay is described by its manufacturers as being ready to use, it will undoubtedly need further preparation – at the very least it should be passed through a pugmill. If you do not have access to a pugmill, you will need to imitate its effects by "wedging" and "kneading" the clay. Some potters only feel happy with their clay when they have continued to wedge and knead it even after it has been pugged.

Wedging

Wedging ensures that the clay is well mixed and also helps to expel any pockets of air which may be present. Small amounts of clay can be "hand-wedged", which simply entails breaking the clay into two, holding the pieces of clay in each hand and smacking them together smartly with force.

This kind of hand-wedging is obviously not practical when you are dealing with large pieces of clay. Wedging large weights of clay involves slamming the whole piece down with considerable, but controlled, force from head height on to a concrete slab positioned at waist height. Once it has been slammed down, the lump of clay should be turned longways and cut in half. One half of the clay is then slammed down from a height on to the other half; this new lump is in turn dissected and one half is slammed down on to the other. This halving and rejoining is repeated until the clay is well mixed and cutting the block in half does not reveal air pockets.

Clay should be wedged until it is quite soft but not sticky. Although you cannot over-wedge clay, wedging does tend to dry clay out and stiffen it. For this reason, bear in mind that the clay you are preparing may need redamping before successful throwing is possible.

1 Hold a piece of clay in both hands at head height and then slam it down with some force on to the concrete slab. Lift the clay and having turned it through 90°, slam it down again. Repeat this process once more.

2 Turn the block of clay lengthways on the slab and slice across it with a cutting wire. Lift one half of this block and slam it down on top of the other. Dissect the clay and re-wedge it.

3 Repeat this slicing in half and rejoining until the clay is thoroughly mixed. If you see any air pockets in the cut surface of the clay, wedge the block again and continue to do so until all the air is expelled.

Kneading

Kneading should take place while the clay is still soft. The two basic methods of kneading take their names from the shape of the clay they create: the "ram" or "bullshead" method and the "spiral kneading" method. Spiral kneading is the best technique to use when preparing large amounts of clay. Downward, forward pressure is exerted on the mass with your strongest hand while you hold, lift and pivot the clay mass on the spot with the other. This serves to offer the next part of the clay to your compressing hand. The action develops a spiral shape in the clay being worked. ▽

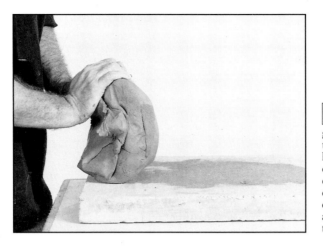

1 The "oxhead" method is probably the easier to grasp, because it imitates the action we associate with kneading dough, although conversely the intention is to expell air. Place your hands close together on the lump of clay and push down and away from your body using the palms of your hands.

2 As the clay spreads away from you, pull the far edge back to the centre in a rhythmic rocking motion. Press down again on the clay that has been pulled back on itself and repeat the process. Spreading the clay over the working surface mixes it and the downward pressure expells any trapped air.

3 The kneaded clay will ultimately look like the head of a bull as a result of this rolling action. Kneading, like wedging, mixes the clay and ensures that it has no air pockets by virtue of the continuous compressing action it involves. ▷

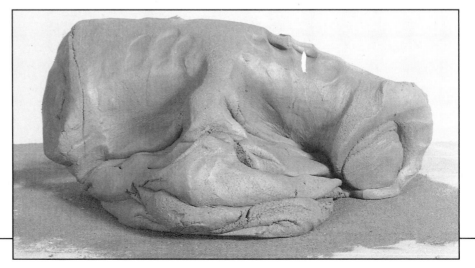

Reclaiming clay

The clay you have to work with may not be in the best condition for throwing. Clay that has dried out too much to use, unfired scraps of clay, and unprocessed clay, can all be reclaimed to use for throwing. Place the clay in a watertight container and pour enough water into it to cover the clay. Leave the clay until it breaks down into a slurry, or has "slaked down". The clay will settle to the bottom of the container. Drain the excess water away. If you are preparing locally dug clay that may have impurities in it, you should pass the slurry through a coarse sieve to remove these foreign bodies.

Remove the slurry from the container and spread it out on a plaster slab or wooden boards so it can begin to dry out. Once the clay has dried sufficiently to be handled without too much of it sticking to your hands, it can be kneaded and wedged ready for use.

Adding other materials to clay

It is often desirable, and in some instances advisable, to add other ingredients or dry materials to plastic clay. Sand or grog are quite common additives which alter the clay's texture as well as its handling characteristics and its final temperature tolerance. In order to mix these into the clay thoroughly while the clay is in its plastic state, the clay mass should be cut into slices, the sand or grog sprinkled between the layers, and then the clay should be kneaded and wedged. Adding dry material to clay dries it out, so additions should be made preferably when the clay is still quite soft.

If colours, in the form of oxide powders or body stains, are to be added to a clay, it is best to mix them with a little water to form a paste. This paste is spread over the slices of clay prior to kneading and wedging. This ensures that the colour is distributed evenly through the clay.

Clay storage

Once clay has been prepared, some form of storage is required that will keep it in prime working condition. Many potters prefer to leave their clay to "age" or "sour" once it has been prepared in order for it to be in peak condition when they come to work with it. Ageing clay simply means that clay in its plastic state is left for a period of time to settle, while souring involves the organic activity of injected bacteria on the clay substance. Although the purist might well insist that clay should be left to age or sour before it

is ready to use, very few aspiring potters have the facilities to store large amounts of clay in order to undertake the processes properly. Luckily, bought plastic clays can be used successfully with the minimum of preparation. In any event, putting clay through a pugmill is considered an effective way to prepare it to the same degree as one month's ageing.

It is the moisture content of a clay that determines its working plasticity so it is very important to prevent water evaporation during storage. Clay manufacturers sell plastic clay in tough polythene sacks and as long as these sacks are not torn, the clay can be kept indefinitely if the sacks are stored in a cool damp environment. Although the effect of frost eventually increases the plasticity of clay, it is a great enemy to any potter trying to store these plastic sacks of clay. Frost tears the polythene sacks causing the clay to spill out, and its initial effect on the clay means that it will need considerable kneading and wedging if it is to be used successfully.

It is always advisable to ensure that sufficient clay is prepared in advance of a throwing session so that your throwing is not interrupted. Smaller quantities of prepared clay are more practical for day-to-day use, and are best stored in plastic bins, with airtight lids. Clay dries out quickly in the warm environment of a studio, so it is advisable not to leave your clay supply exposed during a throwing session.

Having to stop in mid-flow is counterproductive, and if a pugmill is not available, preparing large quantities of clay is both time and energy consuming.

The wheel and the thrower's tools

The most basic potter's wheel is simply a flat turntable fixed to a vertical shaft. The ways in which the shaft causes the turntable, or wheelhead, to rotate and the methods used to power the mechanism have developed over the years to produce a wide range of wheel types. Nevertheless, these wheel types can be roughly categorized into three groups: the "direct kick" wheels; the "treadle kick" wheels; and the electric wheels.

The direct kick wheel consists of a large fly wheel that is rotated by hand or foot. The wheel relies on the weight of the fly wheel to provide a period of continuous rotational momentum during which throwing can take place. The disadvantage of this type of wheel is that it is difficult to control or greatly vary the speed at which it rotates. The treadle kick wheel can be seen as the logical development from the direct kick wheel. The main difference between the two is that instead of kicking the flywheel directly, the potter uses a foot-operated treadle to control its momentum. Wheels of this type are available with either front or side treadles. The front treadle style is operated in a standing position and has a very lightweight flywheel, making it tiring to try and maintain a constant speed for any length of time. This type of wheel is often the cheapest, but its use is limited; beginners especially will find it very frustrating trying to balance on one foot, treadle steadily with the other *and* think carefully about their throwing technique. The best style of treadle wheel is one with the treadle step at the side, such as the David Leach kick wheel. These wheels usually have a flywheel that is sufficiently heavy to maintain a good rotational momentum without excessive effort. They are also operated from a seated position, which eliminates the problems of stance and stability.

Personal preference coupled with many years of teaching has led me to believe that the electric wheel is by far the best option. Although they are more expensive than kick wheels, electric wheels are easy to use and demand the minimum of physical effort. The purist might argue that the electric wheel does not allow for the same sensitivity of control that the kick wheel provides, but this minor drawback is compensated for by the ease with which the electric wheel can reach a range of speeds and maintain them indefinitely. Once you have bought your wheel, it will require very little maintenance to keep it in good working order.

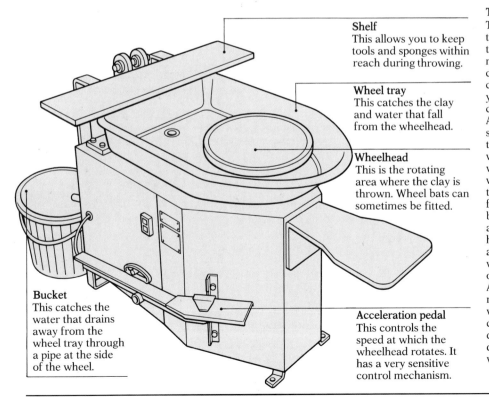

Shelf
This allows you to keep tools and sponges within reach during throwing.

Wheel tray
This catches the clay and water that fall from the wheelhead.

Wheelhead
This is the rotating area where the clay is thrown. Wheel bats can sometimes be fitted.

Bucket
This catches the water that drains away from the wheel tray through a pipe at the side of the wheel.

Acceleration pedal
This controls the speed at which the wheelhead rotates. It has a very sensitive control mechanism.

The electric wheel
There are many different types of electric wheel on the market. It can often be more practical to opt for a cheaper model, so that you can buy all the equipment you need, rather than choose the most expensive. A variety of different systems are used to transfer the motored rotation to the wheelhead — cone systems, variable pulleys, friction wheels and variable transformers to name but a few. The crucial thing to bear in mind when choosing a wheel is that it should have a good range of speeds, and will slow down whatever the speed setting or size of clay being thrown. A mistake often made by new potters is to buy a wheel that suits their initial capabilities, and then discover that this wheel does not function efficiently when their range increases.

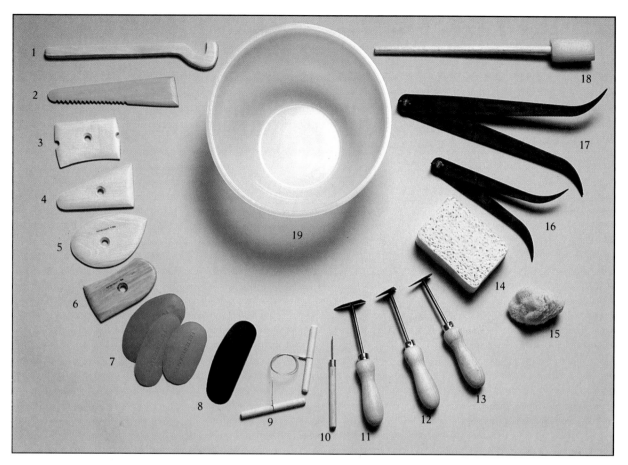

The thrower's tools

The only absolutely essential items needed by a potter are a wheel, clay, water and his hands. There are, however, several tools which assist the throwing process considerably and every potter quickly accumulates a range of items that become personal essentials.

I feel that the most important aid to successful throwing is the removable wheel bat. Although wheel bats may technically constitute equipment rather than tools, I have included them in my discussion of the tools because I see them as an invaluable help when removing large or delicate pieces of work from the wheelhead. If you cannot afford a special system as such, you can make your own by setting two studs into the wheelhead and boring two locating holes through several wooden wheel bats that correspond to the position of these studs. It is essential to ensure that the studs do not protrude above the level of the wood. It is very simple to increase a wheel bat's use further by drawing on several concentric rings: these make invaluable guidelines during turning when accurate re-centring is essential, *(see p26)*.

1-8: Throwing ribs are useful for shaping, smoothing and steadying thrown shapes. A variety of shapes are available in wood, but rubber and metal kidneys can be used for the same purpose.

9: Cutting wire to cut pots from the wheelhead. Twisted wires produce a pleasing shell pattern on the pot base.

10: Needles, preferably set into handles, for trimming off any unevenness from rims.

11: Turning tools are used for paring away unwanted clay from the base of thrown forms, both directly after throwing is completed and at the leather hard stage when the pot is inverted on the wheelhead for turning to take place. These tools are available with a variety of differently shaped working edges. The most commonly used are rectangular, triangular and pear-shaped, but it is always useful to build up a range of shapes.

14,15: Large synthetic sponges for mopping out the wheel tray and general cleaning and small natural sponges for smoothing off finished thrown forms.

16,17: Calipers for recording measurements of rim diameters for lid fittings and other necessary dimensions.

18: Sponge stick for mopping out water from the inside base of tall or narrow-necked forms.

19: Bowls are required to hold the water necessary to lubricate the clay.

Centering

Centring is the process which ensures that the clay is revolving in the centre of the wheelhead. It is the key to successful throwing. All potters eventually develop their own pet throwing techniques to achieve specific results, and by the same token centring is undertaken by different potters in very different ways. Nevertheless, although techniques may differ, the principle remains the same — to align a piece of clay in the exact centre of the wheelhead before throwing begins. I have described several different hand positions for the final stage of centring, which can be adapted until you find the centring position that is most comfortable and successful for you.

Centring is arguably the most important aspect of throwing, because until you have mastered the technique it is unlikely that you will be able to throw effectively. The results of throwing from an uncentred block of clay include walls of uneven thickness, weak spots, and poor and unstable shapes.

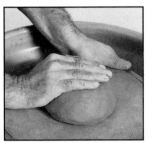

1 It is always best to use soft well-prepared clay to practise centring. Block the clay into a ball and slam it down on to the wheelhead, placing it as centrally as possible. Pat the block into a round domed shape. Make sure you are comfortably seated.

2 Use the edge of the wheel tray to steady your arms as you lean over the wheelhead. Lubricate your hands and the clay with plenty of water. During centring, try to ensure that your hands are linked together for steadiness.

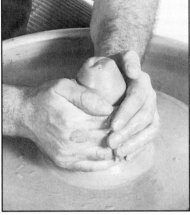

3 Imagine that the circle of the wheelhead is a clock face and place your arms at about twenty past seven. Use pressure from the outer edge of the palms of both hands to force the clay up into a cone.

4 Bring the cone down again by cupping its apex with your right hand, supporting the sides of the form and this hand with your left hand. Repeat the process several times. Coning helps to move the clay into the centre of the wheelhead; it distributes moisture evenly through the clay; and it disperses any air pockets.

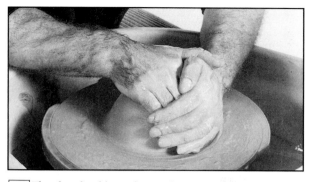

5 The clay should now be nearly centred. There are several final centring positions. Place your arms at half past eight on the wheelhead and cup the clay with both hands. The fingertips of your right hand should touch the surface of the wheel, while your left hand acts as a support. Press down on the clay with your right hand, while pulling towards you simultaneously with your left.

6 With your arms in the same position, apply pressure with your left hand while pushing away from you with your right. Grip your left wrist with your right hand for support.

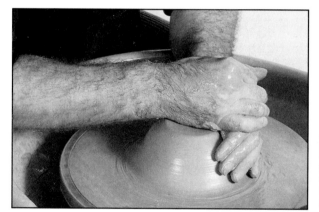

7 Again, with your arms in the same position, press down on to the clay with the outer edge of your right hand while pushing away with your left.

8 Always leave the surface of the clay very gradually — sudden movements may throw the clay off centre. Check that the clay is accurately centred by touching the side of the dome lightly with the point of a tool. If the clay is centred, the circumference line will appear without a break or any unevenness. As your experience increases, you will know instinctively when the clay is correctly centred.

A Cylinder

The two most important basic throwing techniques are employed when making the cylinder and the shallow open form. For a cylinder, begin by practising with small pieces of clay; as your expertise increases, use larger amounts. This step-by-step outline is based on throwing 3.5kg (7lbs) of clay, but 1kg (2lbs) is a good weight with which to practise.

1 Press your thumb into the centred clay to a level about 2 cm (³⁄₄in) above the wheelhead. Support the outer surface of the clay with your left hand and brace your arms against the wheel tray for steadiness. Form the inner base by pushing your thumb out towards the fingers of your right hand. Use your left hand to support the outer wall. △

2 With the clay gripped between your thumb and first finger, keep a constant but gentle pressure and steadily raise the wall to increase the height of the cylinder. ◁

3a

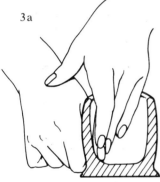

3 During subsequent lifts of the wall, you will find it necessary to substitute the initial lifting grip of thumb and first finger with one that involves both hands. This change becomes necessary when you can no longer reach the surface of the inner base with your thumb. Lift the outer wall with the inner side of your right hand, holding it clenched slightly to form a fist. Support the inner wall with your left hand, pressing with your middle finger against the lifting action of your right.

4 It is important that the lift is a directly vertical one or the shape will flare outwards. You may find it easier to stand leaning over the wheelhead and guide the clay up from that perspective. It is also very important to keep the pressure between your hands constant. If it alters, the form may develop a twist or tilt off balance and the wall may even tear. △

5 Reduce the speed of the wheel and collar the cylinder with steady pressure from both hands. This will steady the clay in readiness for further lifts. To ensure steadiness throughout the throwing process, either rest your forearms on the wheel tray or tuck your elbows into your sides. Movement is minimised because it derives purely from your linked hands.

6 Trim the edge of the rim with a needle. Hold the needle in your right hand and steady the inside of the form with your left, at the point where the clay will be cut. Push the needle into the clay and rotate the wheel slowly. When the needle meets your finger on the inside of the cylinder, lift off the loop of clay. ▷

7 Gently compress the rim to both flatten and thicken it. Use a throwing rib or a suitable turning tool to gently compress the wall of the cylinder for greater stability. Support the inner wall with your left hand as you do so. △

8 Mop out any water remaining inside the cylinder with a sponge attached to a stick. Trim away any excess clay from around the base.▽

How to identify faults

The most common cause of problems when throwing a cylinder is initial inaccuracy in the centring of the clay. If, however, a cylinder develops a swelling midway up its side or in its upper section, the chances are that you are not lifting it vertically and are therefore allowing the walls to flare out, or that your fingers are incorrectly positioned during the lift. If you are exerting pressure with the fingers of your left hand at a point either above or below the corresponding pressure exerted by your right hand, the shape will flare at that point, (see Swelling p23).

If the clay wall tears during a lift, it is usually a result of trying to lift too much in one go and applying too much pressure. Alternatively it could be because you have suddenly increased the pressure at one point. Tearing can also result from lack of lubrication – your hands will stick to the clay if it is too dry and distort or tear it.

A shallow open form

The open form is probably the easiest shape to begin throwing, because the centrifugal force of the rotating wheel almost wills the clay to open out once you start the process. Throwing the cylinder, on the other hand, demands that this tendency to open out be contained and redirected in a vertical direction to give the form height.

1 Centre the clay and spread it out on the wheelhead to form a flattened shape, using the palm of your right hand to press the clay down. Support the widening rim of the clay with your left hand. The area of the wheelhead that the clay covers will determine the width of the base. The maximum diameter of the form can only be a little more than this if the wall is to remain stable. ◁

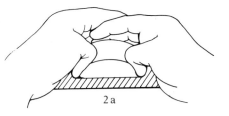

2a

2 Form a small well in the centre of the clay with the tip of your right thumb to a level about 2cm (³⁄₄in) above the wheelhead. Add a little water to the well and place both thumbs inside it. Push both thumbs outwards in opposite directions, supporting the clay with your palms. As the form opens out, maintain a steady pressure on the rim with the inside edge of your thumb to prevent it from splitting. ▷

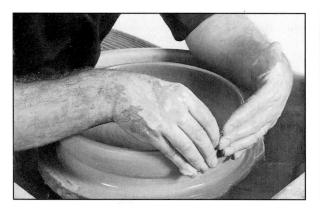

3 Once the diameter of the wall extends the base by about 3cm (1¹⁄₅in), remove any water from the inside of the form with a sponge while it is still rotating. If the wall is thick enough, raise it slightly using your thumb and middle finger. The rim can be compressed to flatten it and if you wish you can also indent it to make it a decorative feature. △

4 Remove some of the excess clay from around the base with a turning tool, ensuring that enough clay is left to maintain the stability of the shape. Cut the shape from the wheelhead with a cutting wire and remove it when it has stiffened, (see *"Removing work from the wheel", p32*).

Swelling

The centrifugal force of the rotating wheelhead encourages thrown forms to open or swell with the minimum of assistance. Consequently the potter is actively engaged in preventing this from happening rather than encouraging it.

When the swelling of a form is required in a controlled manner, however, it is undertaken either as a part of the lifting or raising process, or once any lifting has been completed. Ideally it should begin from the very first lift – the final swell being determined by the tendency of the emerging wall. The final shape only then needs slight modification or refinement towards the end of the throwing process.

1 The forming of a bowl shape shows the swelling technique most clearly since both lifting and swelling occur simultaneously. Begin to develop a gradual swell with your first lift. This is especially important when you are throwing large forms whose stability relies on very gradual and careful swelling. ▷

2 During swelling, pressure should be exerted from within the form with the fingers of your left hand, with your right hand providing support as well as lifting. Further lifting and swelling requires the same hand action. The thickness of clay is now used to swell the shape rather than extend the height of the wall. ▷

3 Modifications in shape can be made using the fingertips of both hands. Any further shaping can take place from within the form. Many potters prefer to use a sponge or a rubber kidney or a rib rather than their fingers. Whenever you are throwing, establish a comfortable, steady position to work from. ◁

4 When you work with small shapes, pressure is still exerted from within, but you may only need the thumb and middle fingers of your right hand to swell the clay. Your left hand acts as a support. △

5 When a shallow swelled form is required, such as in the making of a domed lid, both hands work to produce a lifting and swelling action. Here once again the pressure is exerted from inside the form with the fingers of your right hand steadying and assisting the lifting action.

Collaring

1 Collaring produces a compression of the clay that both thickens and steadies the wall. Consequently, even when you are throwing a straightish cylinder, a very gentle collaring action may be advisable as you raise the shape to stabilize and compress the walls. △

2 When a rounded or completely enclosed shape is being made, we can see quite clearly how pressure from within swells the wall and how pressure from without closes it over. The passive hand is used as a means of steadying the wall as it is manipulated to the desired shape. △

Collaring, or throttling as it is sometimes known, is the term applied to the technique used to restrict or narrow the shape of a form. The action employed in this technique involves gripping the clay with your hands as if you were strangling it. Pressure is applied inwards through both hands as they collar over the specific area to be narrowed. Collaring demands far more from the potter and the clay than does swelling, for instance, because trying to restrict or narrow the shape works against the tendency of the clay to open out as the wheel rotates. It should be carried out in gradual stages with the shape being coaxed rather than forced inwards. The wheel should be rotating at a medium speed and pressure should be exerted in a gentle, determined fashion. During throwing, the ultimate form of any shape should be kept in mind from the start. If a form needs to be tapered or narrow at a particular point, this shaping should occur gradually. Only last minute refinements should be necessary when lifting is completed.

3 Narrowing a shape produces a compressed, thickened section in the clay. This thickening can be used to produce shapes which might otherwise have proved difficult to throw — a round-bellied form with a long narrow neck for example. The neck area is defined by collaring after an initial lift, leaving the neck section thick so that further lifting can take place without altering the shape of the lower section. Repeated collaring allows for more shaping. △

4 Collaring can also be used to produce interesting design effects during throwing. Collaring at intervals up the wall of any shape will alter its silhouette in an unusual way. The extra thickness around the rim area of thrown forms in which collaring results is put to good use when making forms, such as teapots, that require an internal gallery. These galleries can be created easily from the extra thickness of clay. ◁

Rims

The rim of a form, like any other part of it, plays an important part in determining the quality of its final appearance. The most essential requirement of any rim, regardless of its style, is that it should appear to be an integral part of the potter's overall design. Very often, beginners fail to work on the rims of pots they throw with as much energy as the rest of the form, with the result that their rims detract from the overall look of their work. The final shaping of the rim may well be determined to a large extent by the function the form is designed to fulfill, but in any event the design of a form should live in harmony with and enhance its function. All the forces exerted in the lifting of walls during throwing flow upwards, so any unevenness or movement off-centre will manifest themselves mainly at the rim. Trimming off any unevenness with a needle allows for the final shaping of the rim to take place with a clean, even result. Rims can be thick or thin, simple or complex in shape, and it is quite possible to alter the nature of a rim completely to suit a particular requirement, as long as the walls of the form are not too thin. Ideally you should plan the rim as an integral part of the whole shape before you begin to throw, so that it emerges as a natural progression of the form. A simple but useful exercise to undertake is to throw a number of similar cylinders with different rims and see how a different rim affects the look of a pot.

1 To make a thickened, slightly sloping rim, first trim off any unevenness and then, supporting the inside and outside of the shape apply pressure to the rim. This compression can be continued for as long as is necessary to produce a slanted surface to the rim.

2 A compressed rim can be split quite simply using your thumb nail to add interest and texture to a piece of pottery.

3 Applying pressure downwards on the inside of a rim, forcing the clay to slope down and inwards produces a very clean outer edge and gives the pot a modern feel.

4 To produce a flared rim, gently bend the edge of the rim outwards. The edge can be left quite angular on a large flared rim, or extended to be really fine and simple.

5 A tapered rim can be produced by collaring and shaping the sloped surface. Continued shaping can produce unusual rims, with flat inner edges or softened edges.

6 The shape of the rim can be altered by manipulating its edge as if a series of spouts were to be made. This gives the pot a crinkled, and highly textured edge.

Turning

Turning, or trimming, is the process by which excess or unwanted clay is removed from the outer base edge and the underside of a thrown form when it has dried to leather hard. It should not be necessary for turning to be performed on the inside or the rim of a form because these areas should be finished during the actual throwing process. The most important reason for turning is an aesthetic one. Apart from altering the ultimate profile of a shape, turning also allows excess weight to be removed, giving a form the right "feel" in relation to its size.

It is always desirable, however, to keep turning to the minimum. It should be looked upon as a means of adding a final correction to a form, rather than as a means of radically altering its shape. When it is leather hard, clay loses the ability it had during throwing to respond to pressure in a fluid way. Many potters argue that, with the exception of spherical shapes, flat dishes and bowls, which are virtually impossible to throw without leaving a ridge of surplus clay around their base, very little if any turning should be required if a shape has been well thrown.

Turning should only affect the base section of a thrown form. Because the thickness of clay at the base of any form is relatively great, the base area always takes longer to dry than the rest of the form. For this reason, once a piece of work is dry enough to handle without fear of deforming its shape, it should be turned upside down to ensure that the piece dries evenly. Removing thrown pieces from the wheelhead and placing them on paper-covered boards to dry ensures that their bases are not distorted, because they are easily removed from the board without needing to be released with a wire; this clean base cut assists easy turning.

Another way to assist turning is to make a conscious effort to keep the thickness of the bases of the forms you throw constant. A thickness of about 2cm ($\frac{3}{4}$in) is usually suitable for most items. If you are sure of the amount of clay on the base you have to work with, you will be able to gauge how deeply you can trim the base without the constant worry of breaking through the clay shell.

Pots should be trimmed when they are leather hard, because at that stage of drying, the clay can be pared off cleanly. If you trim a pot when it is too damp, the clay trimmings will stick to the sides of the form; if you leave a pot too long, turning will take much longer and the clay will come away as a crumbly powder.

Re-centring

Just as good throwing depends on the clay being centred accurately, successful turning depends on accurate re-centring. It is impossible to re-centre a pot that was thrown when wrongly centred, but you can turn an "off-centred" pot if you concentrate on re-centring its base rather than its rim. Metal wheelheads have concentric rings marked into their surface which can be used to help you re-centre your work. If you are using a wooden removable wheel bat, it is well worth drawing such a guide on to it with a pencil.

1 Simply rotate the wheel slowly and hold a pencil to it to mark out several concentric widths. A pot that was well-centred initially can be easily re-centred using the rings as a guide and will require only slight adjustments. Check that your work is centred accurately by holding a tool steadily against the surface of the form as it rotates. △

2 If the line produced on the form is uneven or broken, re-align your work away from the point where the tool has cut most deeply into the clay. If the line is constant and of an even depth, the pot is centred and you can secure it to the wheelhead. ▷

Turning priorities

A comfortable position at the wheel and body steadiness are as important during turning as during throwing. Whenever possible, rest your forearms on the wheeltray. Turning is best performed with your arms held at half past three on an imaginary clockface. Try to support your trimming hand with your left to provide maximum stability.

The footring is an important feature of any piece and should be considered in advance. The shape and size of a footring will depend on the type of form you throw, but it is always useful to form it so that you can grip it easily with one hand. You will then be able to dip the form in its glaze without losing your grip on its base. ▷

The most common problems to arise during turning are associated with the pot having been incorrectly centred, or with the clay being in the wrong condition to work with. "Chattering" may occur, when the surface of the clay develops ripples, either because the clay is too dry to turn, because you are holding the tool too loosely, or because the tool is not sharp enough. Pots thrown from clays with a heavy grog content will often develop horizontal scratches across their surface. These scratch lines can be eliminated by smoothing with a rubber kidney, a wooden tool or a throwing rib as the wheel rotates.

Not all thrown shapes are stable when inverted, however, and some require special supports during turning. Large bowls with diameters wider than that of the wheelhead, rounded pots with very small necks and pots with long narrow necks all need these supports, or "chucks" as they are known. A chuck can be made from thickly thrown collars of clay that have been left to dry to leather hard. Alternatively, there are many objects that can be used as chucks, such as plastic plant pots, plastic bowls or lengths of sturdy cardboard tubing. Such chucks benefit from the addition of a coil of soft clay around their rims, to cushion the inverted pots.

Turning long-stemmed forms

For a chuck, use a length of sturdy tubing cut so as to prevent any weight pressing on to the fragile lip of the carafe. Alternatively, you could throw a clay chuck. Centre the chuck and secure it to the wheelhead with small pieces of clay. To cushion the inverted carafe, smooth a thick coil of clay around the lip of the chuck and down over the sides. Trim the upper rim of the cushion level with a pin. Trim the base of the carafe and finish in the usual way.

1 Begin the turning process by levelling the base of the form. Brace your arms against your sides. Start at the centre and lightly pare off the clay in even whorls, moving your turning tool out towards the edge. This will remove any unevenness.

2 Trim away any ragged clay from the edge before you define the footring. Trim the outside of the pot to the required profile and define the area in which you want to form the footring. Work from the centre to the inner side of the footring area.

3 Work from the outer side of the footring down over the edge of the base. Pare away the clay gently, resisting the temptation to apply more pressure, which could cause the tool to become embedded in the clay, pushing the pot off-centre or dislodging it.

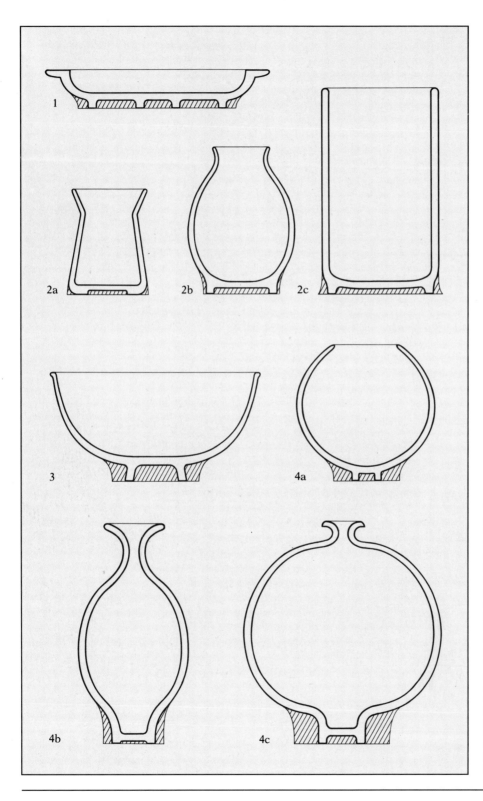

Footrings

These cross-sectional drawings show the shapes of various turned footrings, together with the quantity of clay that has to be trimmed away. Wide dishes require a double footring to prevent sagging *(1)*, while narrower cylindrical forms need only a small amount of trimming to be fully stable, *(2)*. Ideally, footrings should be made so that they are easy to grip when the form is inverted during glazing, *(3)*. Large shapes with swollen bellies should be thrown with relatively thick bases to be stable, and their footrings will therefore need to be trimmed quite substantially before they attain their intended shape, *(4)*.

Handles

Handles for different pieces of pottery can be made by either "pulling" or "extruding" techniques, depending on your personal preference and the style of the pottery you are making.

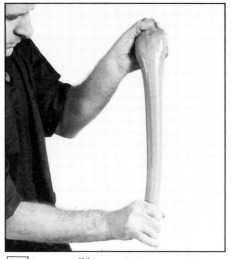

Pulling a handle

1 Pat a large lump of well-prepared clay into a thick carrot shape. Hold the clay comfortably, slim end pointing down. Lubricate your hands and the clay thoroughly and begin to tease the clay down, stretching it with a rhythmic action. Be careful not to increase the pressure applied at any point since this will cause weakness in the handle.

2 As you pull keep twisting your wrist through 180° to ensure that the handle develops evenly. As the handle thins out, alter its shape by changing the position of the fingers of your right hand. Flatten your thumb towards the palm of your hand to form a narrow U-shape.

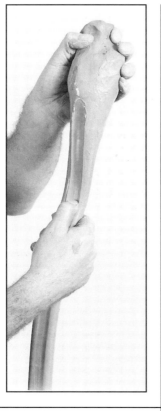

3 Running your hand down the handle in this position will develop a flattened shape. When the handle has thinned down to the correct width to suit the piece for which you have pulled it, run your thumb firmly down the centre to make a shallow groove. The length and thickness of the handle is determined by the object it is to fit, but the principle remains the same no matter what size the handle is to be. Once you are happy that you have pulled enough clay for however many handles you need, divide it up and leave the strips to stiffen slightly before attaching them. You can shape the handles when the clay is still pliable enough to create the sort of shape that you require.

Extruding a handle

Handles can be made very quickly by extruding from a pugmill or extruder. Die plates designed for this purpose can be bought, or made by carefully cutting out a template from a suitable sheet of metal. You can extrude a handle from a block of soft clay with a piece of stiff wire. Bend the wire with pliers to form the sectional shape you need for a handle. Draw the wire, held vertically, through the top layer to the length of the handle you need. The wire will slice through the clay, extruding a shaped segment of clay as it passes through.

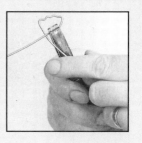

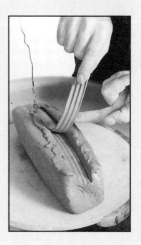

Working with large pieces of clay

Centring

1 Use very well-prepared clay when throwing large forms. Pat the lump of clay into an even, rounded dome to make centring easier. Keep the wheel at a steady rate, slower than that needed to centre smaller pieces of clay. Begin to move the off-centred clay up to the top. The effort required to centre a large piece is not that much greater than that required for a small amount, but it is tiring. Begin to cone the clay. ▷

The sheer exhilaration involved in handling large amounts of clay successfully on the wheel makes this aspect of throwing particularly appealing to most potters. Few enthusiasts can resist the challenge presented to them by large pieces of clay, and a successful end result can promote an enormous sense of achievement.

Even beginners can expect to progress fairly rapidly as they learn to handle large amounts of clay. Any problems are usually the result of a generally poor throwing technique rather than any intrinsic difficulties. A poor technique can often be disguised when throwing small pieces, because structural weaknesses are less noticeable; the opposite is true when throwing large pieces – any shortcomings or mistakes are highlighted and substantially exaggerated.

2 As you push the cone down, keep one elbow braced on the wheel tray and the other tucked into your side. Spend a while centring before you open the clay by pushing your thumb into it. If necessary, use your fist to force the clay to open. Slow the wheel down. △

3 Gripping your hands together begin to form the base and lift the walls. Maintain pressure between your hands and a steadying support as the walls extend. Keep the clay well lubricated, but do not allow it to build up in the base. ▷

Composite forms

Large forms can also be made by assembling several small thrown pieces. These composite forms can be made to a more complex design than a "thrown-in-one" pot, and the method employed is very simple. Each thrown section should be left to stiffen slightly before they are assembled. You must also ensure that the diameters of the rims to be joined together are equal and that the walls of all the forms are equally thick, to avoid uneven shrinkage and cracking at the joint. Centre one section at a time, score its rim, apply slurry and join the next piece.

Throwing coiled additions

The size of the forms you make need only determined by the size of the kiln you have at your disposal. A succession of sections can be added to a slightly stiffened form, thrown, allowed in turn to stiffen and be added to. These extra sections can be added as coils, freshly thrown pieces, or stiffened pieces with a throwable top section.

1 Throw a sturdy base section from the greatest weight you can manage with a levelled, thickened rim and leave it until it has stiffened slightly. Roll a thick, even coil of clay and attach it with slurry to the scored rim of the base section, compressing it into a squared roll. ▷

2 Take particular care to seal the join between the ends of the coil, because this can be a particularly weak area in the clay wall. Smooth the edge of the clay coil down over the rim with your thumb. Leave the coil in place to settle before you begin to throw. Lubricate the clay and begin to throw in the usual way. ▷

3 Concentrate on the top of the base section and the new coil where the clay is most receptive to alteration. Trim the rim and allow this new form to stiffen before repeating the process, should you wish to. △

Combining the Techniques

Throw a sturdy base section on a removable wheel bat. Measure its rim diameter and leave it to stiffen. Do not cut it free with a cutting wire. Throw a second section in the same way with an equal rim diameter and a thickened base. Leave this on the wheel bat to stiffen. Score both rims and re-locate the first form in the wheel. Apply slurry to its rim and attach the inverted second form to it, holding the wheel bat as you do so. Check that the two rims are aligned and smooth the join over. Remove the wheel bat from the top. Cut a hole in the thick base of the inverted form, just large enough for you to insert your hand and throw from the band of clay around the rim of the pot.

Removing work from the wheel

Removing your work from the wheelhead is as crucial an operation as any other part of throwing, since even the best thrown pots can be ruined by careless removal. Just as throwing techniques vary according to the shape of the form being made, personal preference and confidence apart, there are specific methods of removing work from the wheel that are suited to certain forms. Unless, of course, you use a removable wheel bat system, when all you need to do is slice the form free from the wheel bat and leave it until it is dry.

Flooding the wheelhead

1 This is the best way to remove your work if you are not working on a removable bat. Hold a cutting wire taut. It must not be too long because it might cut the base unevenly and make trimming difficult. Press the wire down on the far side of the wheelhead. Slide it towards you, under the pot.

2 Flood the wheelhead making sure that the water does not spill over into the pot. Slice under the pot with the wire again to force the water under the base.

3 Take a wet tile and hold it level with the surface of the wheelhead. The pot will slide on to the tile when pushed from its base. Repeat if it does not move easily.

Direct Lift
Remove any slurry from the outer base of the pot with a rib. Ensure that your hands are dry. Slice under the pot with a cutting wire. Take hold of the form as near the bottom as possible and with a gentle rocking motion, ease it off the wheelhead surface. Once you have mastered this method, you will be able to remove work quickly, and leave a clay pad in the middle of the wheelhead to which the next piece you throw will adhere.

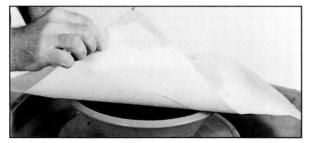

Removing the forms
Cut under the base with a wire and place a piece of paper across the top of the form. Seal its edges to the rim. The paper will trap the air within the form and help it to keep its shape when it is gently lifted off the wheel bat.

Removing delicate forms
Some forms are difficult, if not impossible, to move when they are soft. Drying them off slightly with a hairdryer will help. Ensure that your hands are dry, rotate the wheel and direct the hairdryer on to the clay to stiffen it.

Repetition throwing and sets

Whether they aspire to work in professional production, or whether they simply want to make a single set of coffee mugs, most potters will find it useful to be able to throw a number of items of a similar size and related shape. There are several simple rules to follow during repetition throwing. The first most obvious one is to weigh out the clay in equal amounts. The next is to keep the shape you throw simple so that it is possible to repeat it without too much effort. Although speed is not always essential, taking a long time to try and capture a certain shape can result in tired-looking end results. A simple shape does not have to be a dull or unimaginative shape; it can often be exciting and fresh where complex shapes seem contrived and over-fussy.

While it is easy to produce a template for the profile of any shape to act as a guide when throwing a set, forms thrown in this way can often look suspiciously unoriginal. Obviously it is a matter of personal preference whether or not to rely simply on your hands and a few simple tools, and potters who practise either of these methods may find the alternative completely abhorrent. The crucial thing to remember is that the use of templates will always alter the finish of the form; it will not have a "thrown" surface and may look machine, rather than hand, made.

It is difficult to achieve any real fluidity of shape through repetition throwing if you are only producing half a dozen or so objects. Try to go and watch a professional potter who produces hundreds of similarly shaped items every week, and you will see repetition throwing at its best — each form retains its individuality and yet fits into a batch as one of many.

Sets

Throwing a number of similar forms does not necessarily imply that you have made a set. In a coffee set, for example, the mugs or the sugar bowl will not be the same as the pot or the jug, but the pieces should have enough common characteristics to show that they all go together. Achieving this corporate unity entails careful design consideration at the earliest stages. Although the size of the components vary, their shapes relate to each other in definite ways. It is often true that the components in a set, when examined closely, are unique in design; it is only a general characteristic that distinguishes all the pieces as "belonging". Decoration and the chosen glaze of course assist in the distinction of the pieces you make, and although not within the scope of this book, these should be borne in mind when you make plans to throw a set.

1 Once you have thrown your "pattern" shape, place it nearby at eye level so that you can see its profile from the wheel. There are several types of measuring gauges that can be used to record the dimensions of height and width.

2 Calipers or a ruler, however, are often all that is required. The simplest way to keep a check on dimensions is to set a stick stuck into a piece of clay onto the side of the wheel tray at the height of the first shape.

The Potter's Projects

Salt pigs

Apart from their obvious functional uses in the kitchen, the two basic pig shapes shown in this project — a tall, straight-sided cylinder and a large enclosed form — involve useful techniques to learn from. The forms also lend themselves to many other ideas. The enclosed form, for example, might effectively be adapted to accommodate a trailing plant. With a looped handle it could be suspended.

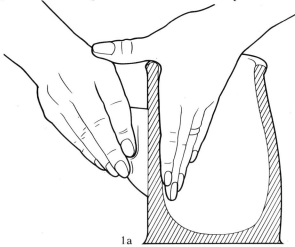

1a

Style A

1 Centre 3.5kg (7lbs) of clay and throw a fairly sturdy cylinder,*(see pp. 20–21)* Once the walls are sufficiently high, trim off the ragged edge of the rim with a needle. Gently press the rim to flatten and thicken it and smooth your throwing rib up the side of the form, supporting from the inside as you go. This will make the surface of the form compact and even, *(see diag)*. Impress a cuff into the rim with the tip of your right forefinger. Smooth the rim with a sponge and mop out any water with a sponge attached to a stick while the wheel is still rotating. △

2 Tidy any waste clay away from the base of the cylinder with a trimming tool and leave the form to dry to leather hard. Hold a cutting wire taut and pull it firmly towards you through the cylinder at an angle of 30°, one third of the way down the form.

3 Score the cut surfaces of both pieces with a knife to ensure a good bond when they are joined with a slurry. Apply the slurry to the edges of both pieces. △

4 Join the pieces together, turning the upper portion through 180° so that when in place it protrudes away at an angle to the main body of the form. Smooth the outer join and place a narrow coil of clay inside it to cover and seal the inner join. Pull a handle and leave it until it has stiffened but pliable. ◁

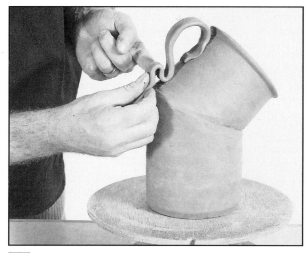

5 Mark the position of the handle on the back of the upper section of the pig. Score this area and apply slurry. Attach the handle, forming a generous curve. △

6 Make the decorative curves at the base and head of the handle with the excess clay pulled for the handle. Bend the strips into loops and smooth the ends on to the body of the pig. Using a wooden scorer, accentuate the position of the handle by incising lines down the sides of the pig. ▷

Style B

1 Again, use 4.5kg (7lbs) of clay. Throw a cylinder of the same size as before, but during the first lift, begin to exert pressure inwards as you approach the top to form a rounded head. ▽

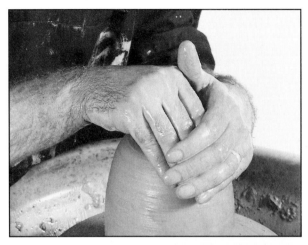

2 Collar the top and △ continue to lift the walls remembering that you will eventually close the top over. Mop up the water inside the form with a sponge attached to a stick.

3 Steady the form with both hands and your arms braced on the wheel tray. Once the walls have thinned out, start to collar at the top until the form actually closes. ▽

4 Remove the excess clay from the top with a pin and seal the wall join over with your fingertips. Once it is sealed, the shape can be modified from the exterior. Trim the excess clay away from the base and smooth up the sides of the form with the throwing rib.

Making the collar

[1] To make the entrance collar, centre 0.6kg (1¼lbs) of clay and flatten it into a low dome. Press the tip of your thumb down through the dome to the wheelhead. Insert both thumbs into this cavity and open the clay. Raise the rim and compress it. For a decorative effect, trim the rim with a needle and lightly indent its flattened surface. Smooth the rim with a sponge, and the walls with the rib. △

[2] Remove the collar from the wheelhead and squash it gently into an oval shape. Leave it until it is leather hard.

Making the knob

[1] To make the knob, centre a small piece of clay and raise it into a small cone. Plumb straight down in the centre of it with your right forefinger until you reach the surface of the wheelhead. △

[2] Raise the wall by gripping the clay between the forefinger and thumb of your right hand. Support the outside wall with your left hand, and gradually collar the shape over. Close the top of the hollow inner column to form a central bulge.

[3] Create a comfortable grip on the knob by squeezing gently around the middle section of this small column.

Final Construction

1 To attach the entrance collar, mark the surface of the form with the base of the oval. Shape the inner surface of the oval collar at an angle so that it fits snugly over the curve of the form. △

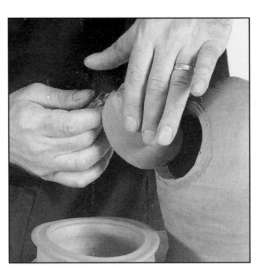

2 Cut out a slightly smaller oval shape from the wall of the form, using the mark on the clay surface as a guideline. Score both the surfaces to be joined and apply slurry. Press the oval collar in place on the form. Tidy up the inside of the entrance with a knife or a finger and smooth the join over with your fingertips. Smooth the outer join in the same way. Wipe over the joins, inner and outer, to ensure that they are well sealed.

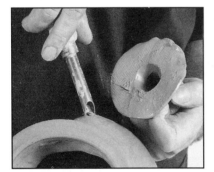

3 To attach the knob, make a hole in the apex of the form with a piercing tool to release the air pressure inside the form, and place the knob over it. △

4 Ease the flared outer lip of the knob down on to the pig and shape it with your fingers to create a fluted effect. ◁

5 Impress the sides of the pig with a wooden roller to add interest to its surface. To complete the decoration of the pig, add small pellets of clay at the base of each indent around the pig and smooth them up with your forefinger to form a petal decoration.

Salt pigs

Very attractive results can be obtained by pouring a lighter
glaze over a darker one. When one glaze is poured over
another, as in this instance, you must ensure that the final
glaze is not too thick or it will run during firing.

Spice jars

The interesting aspect of these jars is that lid and base are thrown as one form. There is no reason why you should not use the same technique to make jars of different sizes. You could also alter the proportions of the lid and knob in relation to the size of the jar. The technique is ideal for making shallow pill-boxes, without incorporating a knob into the design.

1 Centre 1kg (2lbs) of well-prepared clay and throw a straight sided cylinder. With consecutive lifts, begin to close the shape in. You will need to raise the form to a higher level eventually, but try not to open out the neck as you do so.

2 Use two fingers of your left hand within the shape instead of your whole hand, resting your remaining fingers on your supporting right hand. Mop out any water using a sponge on a stick while the wheel is still rotating.

3 Because the shape has been collared, there will be plenty of clay to work with in the upper section of the pot. This extra thickness will be important when you start to form the knob. Close the form over when the walls are the right height.

4 The pressure exerted against the clay walls by the air trapped within the form allows you to mould the pot without worrying that the form will collapse. Begin to shape the knob by collaring gently at the apex of the pot.

5 Make sure that the walls of the pot are straight in the section where the lid will eventually meet the base. Use a rib to straighten off any unevenness in this area and smooth down the clay. Remove any waste clay from the base.

6 Using a small rectangular piece of wood, start to dig into the wall at the point where you want the lid segment to begin, forming a smooth indentation. Use a rib to ensure that the walls of the pot and lid are level. Even off any ragged edges and leave the pot to dry to leather hard.

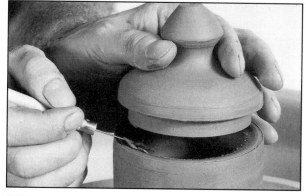

7 Recentre the pot, securing it with small pieces of clay. When the piece dries it will shrink and the air pressure inside it will build up and may distort the form. To prevent this, pierce the side of the form with a needle. Use the needle to cut through the wall at the point where the pot juts out under the indentation to release the lid.

8 Trim off the rim of the pot with a needle. Use the pot cavity as a chuck for trimming the lid.

9 Invert the lid into the pot and secure it with small pieces of clay. Trim off any ragged edges on the lid flange with a trimming tool to ensure that the lid fits into the pot.

10 Put the lid the right way up on the pot and trim the walls flush. At this stage you can also shape the knob and make a decorative feature of the lid's rim by trimming into the swell.

11 Turn the base of the jar and pare off its edges at an angle of 45°. Hollow out a central indentation and smooth the whole jar off with a sponge.

Spice jars

A warm-coloured glaze would seem to be the most
appropriate for a set of jars which contain various spicy,
tangy substances. The shiny finish provides an extra touch
of luxury.

Cheese dish

1 To make the cover of the dish, centre 2.5kg (5lbs) of clay. Flatten the clay out until you reach the circumference you want to work to. Push your thumbs down through the clay to the wheelhead and open the form.

The technique used for making the cover of the dish can be adapted to make a plant container, hung upside down in a macramé hanging, or even a large lid for a meat dish, with the addition of a separately formed handle.

2 When the clay ring is about 1.3cm (½in) thick, begin to raise the walls. You should aim to produce a rounded bell-shape. As you near the top, reach into the form through its narrowed opening to finalize the swelling. ▷

3 Collar the top of the form, producing a good thickness of clay from which to develop the handle. Ensure that the handle you throw affords a good grip. Trim off any unevenness on the rim with a needle. If you wish you can close the open end of the handle with a small pellet of clay. ◁

4 Smooth off the outer walls of the cover using a rib. Trim away any waste clay from the base and use your trimming tool at the same time to accentuate the lower lip of the cover. ▷

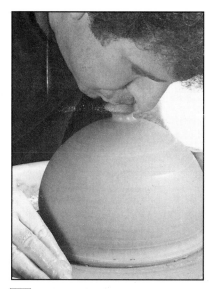

5 You can inflate the dome shape of the cover by blowing gently into it through the handle spout to produce an even shape. Measure the diameter of the cover so that you know how wide to make the dish. The lid will sit inside the rim of the dish. △

6 Trim the cover once it is leather hard. Invert it into a plastic basin that has been secured to the wheelhead with small pellets of clay. Roll a thick clay coil and wrap it around the rim of the cover to cushion it during trimming.

7 To finish off the cover, paint bands of different widths around it with coloured slip. Firstly, paint a wide band of thick slip around the middle section of the cover. Then with a fine brush paint slimmer decorative lines around the rim, the lip of the handle and the top of the cover bell.

8 Using a piece of stiff card or hardboard with teeth cut into one end, rotate the wheel and scratch a surface pattern into the slip before it dries. The scratching will expose the lighter colour of the clay beneath the slip and produce an attractive design. Brush off any excess slip scratchings when the cover has dried.

Making the dish

1 To make the dish, centre 2kg (4 lbs) of clay. Begin to spread the clay, checking the diameter measurement as you do so. Form a low ridge around the circumference of the flattened shape.

2 Steady the outer wall of the ridge as you establish the dish shape. Once you have reached the required diameter, refine the shape of the dish.

3 Use a throwing rib to develop a good, firm shape. The rib smooths the surface of the dish and gives clear-cut edge to its inner curve.

4 Bend the rim of the dish gently outwards, supporting the base of the form with your left hand as you ease over the clay with your right.

5 Having smoothed the dish and trimmed away any waste clay at its base, leave it to dry to leather hard. Using coloured slip as described on p. 47, you can decorate its rim with a design that complements the cover.

Cheese dish

A darkly coloured slip can usually be relied upon to bleed
through a light coloured glaze such as the one used to
complete this piece. The slipped combed pattern, although
slightly obscured by the glaze, remains visible.

Eggcup stand

When they are examined, many seemingly complex forms prove to be no more than a combination of simple shapes. This egg cup stand combines simple throwing skills to produce an unusual functional item.

1 | Centre 3.5kg (7lbs) of clay. Open the clay out with the tips of both thumbs, keeping the emerging base flat, until it almost reaches the width of the wheelhead. Steady the clay wall with your palms. ◁

2 | Lift the thick clay collar around the edge of the flattened base. Continue to raise the wall, maintaining reasonable thickness on the emerging rim. The rim will ultimately support the inverted form so it is important that it is kept as sturdy as possible.

3 | Trim off any uneveness before compressing the rim. Remove any water from within the form with a sponge and trim away any excess clay from around the base. △

4 | Once the form has dried to leather hard, invert and centre it on the wheelhead, and secure it with small clay pellets. Begin to turn the base, remembering that the surface you are smoothing down is actually the top surface of the form. Work outwards flattening the clay and leave a small ridge around the edge of the upper area. Smooth the form with a damp sponge.

6 The holes should be made slightly larger than is necessary because they will shrink during firing. Cut out the holes, starting them with a piercing tool and finishing with a needle. Angle the sides of the cuts slightly and smooth them with a sponge. Tidy the inside of the stand.

5 The six holes in which the egg cups will sit should be cut out at regular points around the circumference of the stand. To divide the circular area into six, take a piece of string and wrap it around the rim of the form, then divide the string, by folding, into sixths. Place a sixth of the string length as a measuring guide around the circumference and mark the clay either side of it. Score lines across the surface of the stand, joining each mark around the circumference with its opposite number. These lines divide the circle up into six equal parts. Each line will exactly bissect the holes made for the egg cups. Draw around a suitable circular object to mark out the six holes. △

Alternative Designs

There are various styles of handle that would be suitable for this stand – basket handles at each side of the form or a single handle bridging its width for example. Extrude several handle lengths from soft clay. For the "bridge-style" handle, flatten the clay length and loop it across the stand, dipping it to join the stand at the exact centre. Score the appropriate areas of both stand and handle, apply slurry and press the handle firmly into place.

For the basket handles, shape two suitable handle lengths. With slurry, attach them to opposite sides of the stand. Angle the handles to point slightly upwards.

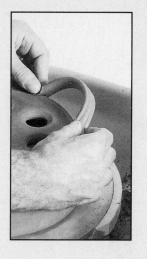

Making the handle

1 Centre 350g (12oz) of clay and throw a small cylinder, plumbing down to the wheelhead with your thumb. Once the basic cylinder shape has emerged, you can shape it as you wish, remembering to ensure that the shape you produce is comfortable to grip. Trim around the base of the knob, reflecting the angular quality of the base. Smooth over the whole form with a damp sponge.

2 When the knob has dried to leather hard, score the central area of the stand where it is to be attached, apply slurry and press the knob firmly into place. Smooth the join over using a wooden tool to firmly seal the edge of the knob to the surface of the stand. ▷

Making the egg cups

1 The matching egg cups are made by stack-throwing. Centre a piece of clay of a size that you can comfortably manage on the wheel and begin to throw a series of small bowls. Keep their rims to a delicate thickness and ensure that they are large enough to hold an egg.

2 Shape the foot of each bowl before slicing it from the stack of clay so that the cups have good stems.

Trim around the swell of the cups once they have dried to leather hard so that they fit snugly in the stand.

Egg cup stand

A rust-coloured glaze has been used on this piece of work.
Wax resist emulsion was then brushed over the surface to
produce a simple pattern and a lighter shiny glaze was
applied.

Hors d'oeuvres tray and dishes

A simple shallow open form is arguably one of the easiest forms to throw on the wheel. Once centred and opened, one simple lift of the wall is required and since it has a low profile, no problems with stability should arise. With a little ingenuity, however, even this simple form can be used to good effect.

1 Centre 4.5g (9lbs) of clay. Once it is centred, spread the clay out on the wheelhead to form a flattened shape using the palm of your right hand and supporting the widening outer rim of the clay with your left. Spread the circular disc wide enough to form a generous tray base, but keep it thick so that a wall can be lifted around its circumference.

2 Open the form out with both thumbs, supporting the clay as it spreads with your palms. Push outwards evenly within the cavity. Press down on the growing rim with your left thumb to prevent it splitting.

3 Continue working the rim out until it protrudes about 2.5cm (1in) beyond the base. Mop out the water in the cavity with a sponge. Lift the rim wall very slightly and straighten it.

4 When the rim is sufficiently formed, compress the outer lip of the tray. To make a feature of the rim, part split it with your fingernail. Smooth the indentation formed with a damp sponge to make a rounded edge. Remove any excess clay from around the base, remembering as you do that the base has to be wide enough to support the tray.

5 Mark out quarters around the edge of the tray with your fingertip as the first step towards reshaping the tray. Once your four "corner" marks are in place, gently tease the rim outwards with your right forefinger at each of these four points — almost as if you were making a spout. Support the clay wall with the thumb and finger of your other hand as you go. This decorative moulding defines the areas within the tray in which the dishes will ultimately fit. As an alternative, you can angle these curves inwards. Once the clay has stiffened slightly, the shape can be reinforced to ensure a well-defined shape.

7 Take two sections of pulled handle and attach them in generous loops to opposite sides of the tray's rim between two curved corners.

6 When the tray has dried to leather hard, invert it on to the wheelhead and secure it with clay pellets. turn the base as usual to ensure that the under surface is well flattened. A wide shallow form requires two supporting footrings to prevent it sagging. Define the position of the two rings with the point of a turning tool and work them up, starting at the outer edge. Smooth off the surface with a sponge.

8 Add extra looped lengths of the pulled handle for a decorative touch at each end of both the handles. If you wish, incorporate a few clay pellets into the decorative scheme. Smooth the handles with a damp sponge.

Making the dishes

1 The four hors d'oeuvres dishes are each made from 0.5kg (1lb) of clay. Once the clay is centred, flatten it down into a domed shape.

2 Make a simple shallow form and raise the walls very slightly. Gently flatten the rim and impress a slight ridge in it with your fingernail, so that the design of the dishes echoes that of the tray. Smooth off the rim.

3 Trim away any excess clay around the base of the dish. When you have sliced the dish off the wheelhead with a wire, gently compress its circular shape into a triangle. This is important if the dishes are to fit snugly into the tray.

4 Once the dishes are leather hard, you can pare off any unwanted clay from the base edges with a sharp knife.

Hors d'oeuvres tray and dishes

A simple opaque white glaze was used on the tray and the matching dishes. Iron oxide has been brushed over the rim surfaces of the tray and all the dishes to accentuate their design details.

Teapots, cups and saucers

When making a tea-set, a single overall design has to be kept in mind when you begin to throw any one of its components. The shape of the teapot should relate to that of the cups and saucers. Two types of teapot construction are described in this project, both with a different lid fitting. The character of the teapot can be altered completely by the style of its lid. These lid fittings can be used for a variety of different forms.

Teapot A

1 Centre 2kg (4lbs) of clay for the body of the pot. Begin to encourage a rounded shape as you raise the wall of the clay, modifying the swell as the wall grows. ◁

2 Begin to curve and close the upper section over by easing the clay gently from within the form. Sit back from the wheel to check that the shape is balanced and developing as required. Finalize the swell of the pot by lifting the clay out and up from the bottom of the form.

3 Collar the neck of the pot, impressing a ledge on which the cup lid will rest. Remove any water from within the form. Throw the thickened rim of the ledge so that a narrow upper wall emerges. Trim off the rim with a needle or a pin. △

4 With a lubricated throwing rib, define the walls of the upper section and the ledge so that the lid will fit snugly over the top. Trim any excess clay from around the base.

5 Measure the exterior diameter of the rim using calipers so that you know the right measurement for the inner diameter of the cup lid when you come to throw it.

6 When the teapot has dried to leather hard, turn any excess clay from its base using a trimming tool. This stage also refines the profile of the pot.

Decorating the teapot

This teapot will look even more attractive with some simple decoration – fluting for example. This decoration is best applied when the walls of the teapot are soft leather hard, before you attach the spout. Fluting undertaken at this stage minimizes the risk of deforming the pot and produces cleaner lines.

Define the area of the pot to be fluted by marking lines circling the sides, (right). Use a fluting tool – a length of wood pared flat at one end will do just as well – and press it into the side of the teapot at the level of the lower line. Gently draw the tool up the side of the pot, either straight or at a slant, (far right), until

you reach the upper line. The clay will peel off in strips. Smooth over the pot with a damp sponge. This decoration will add interest to any style of teapot you choose to make.

Making the lid

1 Centre 170g (6oz) of clay and throw a very small bowl. Check the inner diameter measurement and stop opening the clay when you reach the right width.

2 Raise a low wall around the shape and thicken its rim as a precaution against chipping. Smooth off the edges with a damp sponge.

3 Trim away any excess clay around the base to refine the curved shape. At this stage you can define the lid's eventual silhouette by trimming tight into the base of the bowl form.

4 When the lid is leather hard, secure it with clay pellets to the trimmed throat of the teapot and refine its curved shape. The lid should be trimmed until it is a good shape to handle easily.

Making the spout

1 The spout can be made when the pot and lid have dried a little because it will dry at a much faster rate. Centre 170g (6oz) of clay and form it into a cone. Plumb straight down to the wheelhead and begin to throw a thin conical cylinder.

2 With each lift thin out and collar the top section of the cylinder, keeping the whole form as slim as you possibly can, but retaining width at the base.

3 With one finger, continue to lift and collar the rim. If the opening is too narrow to insert a finger, use a dowel or the handle of a brush.

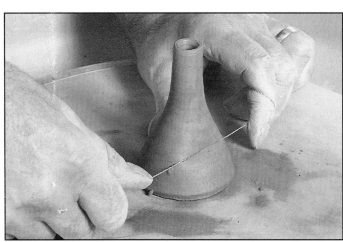

4 Flare the rim of the spout slightly. Trim away any waste clay from the base and leave it to dry to soft leather hard. To attach the spout, slice away a portion of its base at an angle. Measure the spout up with the body of the teapot to check its proportions and where to attach it.

5 The end of the spout should not be lower than the level of the lid, or tea will pour out as the pot is filled. Trim the sliced surface of the spout so that it fits smoothly on to the teapot. Once you are happy with the position of the spout, mark the teapot around the edge of it's base.

6 Using a piercing tool held at 45°, make several straining holes within the marked spout area. Score the cut surface of the spout and the marked area on the teapot. Apply slurry and attach the spout. Blow down the spout to unblock it. △

7 Smooth off the join between the two pieces using any suitable tool and a sponge. If necessary, add a coil of clay around the join and smooth it into place. Gently mould the bottom edge of the spout.

Alternative Spouts

The end of the spout can be left as it is or it can be trimmed at a gentle angle using a taut wire. If you do slice off the end at an angle, slant your cut slightly to the left to counter the slight twist that firing will inevitably give to the spout.

Complete the shaping of the spout by easing the lower lip of the newly cut edge down. This angling of the lip assists pouring.

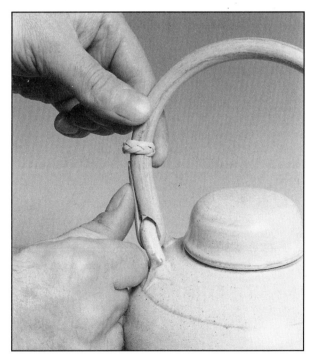

This style of teapot looks very attractive with a cane handle. Extrude or roll out two short coils of clay. Site the area directly above the teapot's spout in line with the centre of the lid and score it. Apply slurry to the ends of one of the coils and press it in place to form a loop over the spout. Repeat this process at the back of the teapot. Smooth small clay pellets over the joins to reinforce them.

Teapot B

1 Centre 2kg (4lbs) of clay and throw a full-bodied pot as you did for teapot A. Remove any water from within the pot before you narrow its throat too much. Collar and compress the rim simultaneously to ensure that it is thick enough for the lid to rest on.

2 Compress the wall of the pot using a throwing rib to smooth down the clay and strengthen the form. Trim away any excess clay from around the base.

3 Measure the diameter of the pot's throat so that you know how large to make the lid. The lid slot that sits within the throat will correspond with this measurement; the ledge of the lid will need to be about 1cm ($\frac{2}{5}$in) wider. △

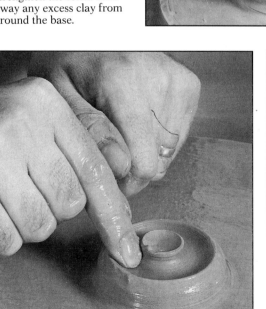

Making the lid

1 Centre 170g (6oz) of clay and open it by pressing into it with your forefinger at a point about 1cm ($\frac{2}{5}$in) from the centre. A small pillar of clay will begin to emerge; the knob of the lid. ◁

2 Widen the outer edge of the lid and raise the wall slightly. Keep a careful check on the growing diameter as you throw and stop opening the shape once you have extended the edge of the form to the required measurement. △

4 Finish shaping the knob with your forefingers, increasing the size of its top to ensure that the lid can be easily gripped. Smooth the lid off with a sponge and trim away any excess clay from the base. Leave it to stiffen before you finalise any trimming and shaping. ▷

3 Begin to flatten and extend the outer wall of the lid over your right forefinger, keeping that finger steadily against the side of the lid to stop it spreading. Once the ledge has reached a suitable width, trim around its edge with a needle and smooth and compress its edge simultaneously with a damp sponge. △

5 Trim the teapot and lid once they are soft leather hard. The footring should be made fairly wide. Centre the teapot the right way up and secure it. Trim the neck of the pot so that the lid sits in it comfortably. Invert the lid, resting it carefully on the thickened pot rim, and secure it with clay pellets. Trim up the underside of the lid to ensure a neat fit. Throw a spout and attach it in the usual way. ◁

Attaching the handle

1 Extrude a handle to a suitable length. Score the area where the handle is to be joined to the pot, remembering to keep the spout, knob and handle aligned. Form the curve of the handle by lining it up with the teapot, and balancing its shape to the pot's swell. Apply slurry to the scored areas and attach the handle. △

2 Ensure that the joins are well bonded, reinforcing them with small rolls of clay. Press these rolls into the body of the teapot, and smooth the joins over with a sponge. △

3 To prevent the handle drooping as it dries, invert the teapot on a flat surface with the handle's upper curve hanging over the edge. ▷

Teapot C

1 Centre 2kg (4lbs) of clay and again throw a round-bellied pot, this time with a thickened rim. Lift a low wall around the rim. Compress it slightly and then split it with your fingertip, using your left hand to support your right.

2 Using a suitable implement, carefully push the inner side of the split clay down into the neck of the pot to form an internal gallery. Smooth off and adjust the shape of the rim above the gallery. Turn the teapot once it has dried to leather hard.

2 With your thumb nail, split the rim and extend the outer edge to form the flange; trim its edge with a needle. Raise the inner wall and form a slight spout to keep the lid in place when it is sitting in the throat of the teapot. Trim the wall so that it is slightly smaller than the width of the teapot; this ensures that it is easy to lift in and out.

Making the lid

1 Centre 170g (6oz) of clay and open it out, retaining a thick outer edge. Measure the diameter to check that you have reached the correct width before you begin to make the flange.

3 When the lid is leather hard, trim it down and add a knob. Begin to trim away the clay moving from the centre of the lid to its edge. When you have trimmed it down to a dome shape, define a circular area over the apex. Score this circle and apply a little slurry over the clay. The knob will be thrown from a lump of clay attached at this point.

4 Score the base of a small cone of clay and attach it over the scored area of the lid. Smooth down the clay to make a firm join. Extend and shape the knob until it is the right size to grip easily. Pierce the lid above its internal lip. Attach a spout and a handle to the teapot as usual.

Making the teacups

1 For each cup, centre 0.2kg (½lb) of clay. Lift up a small dome with a narrow base. Begin to open out the dome, bearing in mind the shape of the teapot.

2 As the walls swell and grow, keep the foot of the cup reasonably narrow. The rim of the cup should be thick enough to withstand everyday wear and tear, but slim enough to be pleasant to drink from. Gently compress the rim with your fingertip. Trim away any excess clay from the base.

3 Measure both the diameter of the cup's foot and the diameter of its rim. The smaller measurement will act as a guide for the central indentation in the saucer, and the larger as a guide from which to work out the final diameter of the saucer. The saucers will be 6.8cm (2½ins) wider than the widest diameter of the cups.

Making the saucers

1 For each saucer, centre 395g (14oz) of clay. Press the clay down into a shallow flattened disc and begin to open it. Check the cup diameter measurement as you go.

2 Begin to lift the edges of the disc into a gentle curve. Do not raise this rim too much; you must leave enough space for the handle of the cup. Smooth the shape with a sponge, thickening the edge as you do so. Using a suitable tool roughly mark out the central area for the cup to stand in.

Trimming the cup and saucer

1 When the cup has dried to leather hard, invert it on to the wheelhead and secure it with clay pellets. Trim the foot of the cup and take an accurate measurement of its diameter as a guide for making the saucer's indentation. ◁

2 When the saucer is leather hard you can finalise any trimming. Secure the saucer to the wheelhead and carefully pare away the clay from the centre to create an indentation of the required diameter. ▷

3 Then invert the saucer and turn its base to reduce its weight and refine its shape. Keep the footring narrow, but wide enough to keep the cup and saucer stable. Smooth over the surface of the saucer with a damp sponge.

Attaching handles to the cups

Extrude suitable slender handles for the cups. Judge the right size of the handle loops by lining them up with the cups, (*top*). Apply slurry and press them into place in the usual way, smoothing the ends into the surface of the cups.

Teapots, cups and saucers

The glaze you choose for the teapots will alter their
appearance in the same way that variations in lid, handle
and spout design do. The decoration of the cups and saucers
should echo that of the pot.

Soup tureen and bowls

The bowl shape is one of beautiful simplicity and need not be difficult to throw. The best bowls, however, have a look of rounded fullness about them which seems to spring upwards from the foot. Regardless of size, the throwing technique is relatively simple, with the centrifugal force from the rotating wheelhead almost willing the shape to open out on its own. Consequently, only very gentle pressure is usually needed to swell the shape evenly.

1a

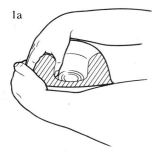

1 Centre 6kg (12lbs) of well-prepared clay to make the bowl. Open the clay and raise and swell the walls gently. Continue to exert pressure outwards as you lift, once the shape begins to emerge. ▷

2 Bring up the thickness of the clay at the base of the bowl to add height to the form, but do not thin it down too much and reduce the basal support. ▷

3 Once you have created the basic form, you can refine and modify it from within, carefully supporting the outer wall. Link up your hands when possible to maximize support. △

4 Trim the rim of the bowl with a needle to remove any unevenness. Compress the rim to give it a firm edge: this helps to stop the edge of the bowl chipping. Use a kidney to shape inside the bowl. Keep your hand steady as you do this by using your left hand to create a supporting bridge, bracing your arm into your sides. Trim away any waste clay.

5 Measure the diameter of the bowl with calipers so that you know how large the lid should be. Once it is leather hard, the bowl can be trimmed.

6 Invert the bowl, centre it on the wheelhead and secure it with clay. Trim the base flat, working from the centre outwards. Next, trim the edges and mark on the guidelines for the footring. Begin to shape the ring, working from the outer edge first.

7 Move to the centre and pare away the clay until the ring emerges. Smooth the base off with a sponge.

8 While the bowl is still leather hard you can attach its handles or lugs. Carefully mark around the handle curves on the sides of the tureen and score both these areas, and the underside of the lugs. Apply slurry and firmly mould the lugs on to the form.

9 Draw the ends of the lugs together into a loop and sweep the flattened ends across each other and around the curve of the bowl. Carve the edges of the curves with a wooden scorer for additional emphasis.

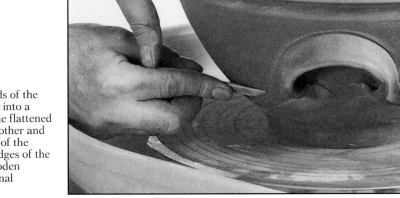

1a

Making the lid

1 To make the lid of the tureen, centre 4.5kg (9lbs) of clay. Spread the centred clay into a wide-based dome of the required diameter. Open out the form, keeping a check on the width.

2 Continue to open out the form measuring its width with calipers from time to time. Begin to raise and shape the emerging wall as you enlarge the diameter.

3 Compress the rim to strengthen it and begin to split it with your fingernail. Trickle water down over your left hand to lubricate the clay and begin to press the outside edge of the rim gently downwards, supporting it underneath as the clay spreads to form a slim flange.

4 Define a 90° angle using a suitable tool. Mop out any water inside the form and smooth the flange with a sponge or strip of chamois leather.

5 Once it has dried to leather hard, invert and centre the lid on the wheelhead. Trim away the clay to emphasize its domed shape, working down over the slope of the lid. Remove the most clay from the area corresponding to the point where the interior curve bends up to meet the rim: the area where the clay is at its thickest.

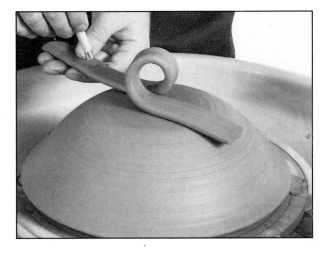

6 When the lid is still leather hard you can attach a handle at its apex. As well as being functional, handles can also be decorative and a style that is particularly attractive for a lid of this kind is a sturdy loop. Smooth both ends of the handle and swing them round to form a central loop. Score the area of the lid to which you are attaching the handle, and the underside of the handle itself. Apply slurry and join.

7 Once the handle is in position, you can incorporate it into the overall decorative design of the tureen. Split the two ends of the handle and spread the splits apart. Smooth the end handle clay down and around the lid, emphasizing the curve of the form as you go. Accentuate the curves using a wooden scorer.

8 Cut out a deep semi-circle from the edge of the lid to allow the ladle handle to sit inside the tureen. Smooth off the edges of your cut.

Making the bowls

1 To accompany the soup tureen, you can make several small bowls. Centre 0.7kg (1½lbs) of well-prepared clay for each bowl and begin to work it up into a shape that reflects the form of the soup tureen.

1a

2 Begin by keeping the base of the bowl fairly narrow, and flare it out as you raise the wall. Keep plenty of thickness at the rim, to echo the edge of the tureen. When you have thrown the bowl to the right height, compress the rim.

3 Modify the shape of the bowl and refine its rim by paring the clay from the walls gently with a trimming tool. Trim away the waste clay at the base of the bowl to give the bowl a clean silhouette.

Making the ladle

1 For the ladle, throw a small round dish using 0.7kg (1½lbs) of clay. Keep the shape sturdy and the rim fairly thick.

2 To make the pouring lip, slightly lift up a section of the lip with your thumb and forefinger. Pull the lifted clay outwards a little, keeping the wall of the ladle bowl steady with your other hand. Form a spout as you would on a jug.

3 Press the ladle bowl very gently to give it a slightly oval shape. Leave it to dry until it is leather hard.

4 The handle for the ladle should be left until it is still pliable but firm enough to maintain a long straight section. Once any trimming is complete, the handle can be fitted. Gently curl the end of the handle to form a good sized grip. Attach the handle with slurry having scored the surfaces to be joined.

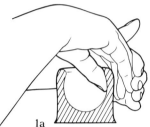

1a

Punch bowl and cups

1 The same methods can be used to make a punch bowl and cups set, but the cups will have to be made in a slightly different way. Use the same weight of clay as you did for the soup bowls, but when you begin to lift the form, remember to keep it narrower at its base — the cups need to be easy to hold.

2 Begin the cup from a narrow cone and allow it to rise straight for about 5cm (2in) before you begin to spread the cup out. As you pull the cup out, keep your arms braced on the wheel tray.

3 Compress and flare the rim slightly to give the cup a pleasant drinking edge. Trim in the base stem considerably to produce a slender stem shape.

4 You can make the punchbowl in the same way as you did the base of the soup tureen, without adding the lugs at the sides or throwing a lid. The ladle to serve the punch will be made in the same way.

Punch bowl set

A light, smooth textured glaze is probably the best choice for
this set, so that whatever the colour of your punch, it will
still look good. A dark brown glaze and cobalt oxide were
used for the pattern.

Casseroles

Style A

1 Centre 2.5kg (5lbs) of clay and open it out to the diameter you require for a casserole. Keep the base of the form fairly wide as you raise the walls. Swell the sides of the form keeping a good thickness of clay around the rim. △

Any item that requires the addition of separate components, such as lids, spouts or handles, should be designed with these components in mind. Casseroles are no exception, but there are also other equally important considerations to bear in mind when making them. Their shape must be stable and easy to serve from, and their handles or knobs must be easy to grip, even through an oven glove.

2 Impress a cuff around the top of the casserole, to define a ridge below its rim and give it shape. Remove any water from within the casserole and trim any waste clay away from the base. Measure the diameter of the rim with calipers so that you know how wide to make the lid. △

3 When the casserole has dried to leather hard, invert it on the wheelhead and secure it with clay pellets. Turn the base, remembering that the footring should be wide enough to ensure that the casserole is stable. ◁

Making the lid

1 Centre 1.2kg (2½lbs) of clay and flatten it out to the diameter of the pot's rim. Open the clay, pushing your thumbs down to the wheelhead. Raise the walls of the form, tapering them at a point about 1.2cm (½in) above the wheelhead. Tease out a low ledge from the wall of this conical shape. ▷

2 To complete the lid, you have two options. You can collar the top of the conical cylinder, narrowing and refining its shape until it forms a knob that is easy and comfortable to grip. ◁

3 Alternatively you can seal the form over completely and then depress the dome of clay, forming a lid with a sunken centre.

4 Pierce the lid with a needle. This will release the air trapped with the form the clay and allow for further depressing of the central area.

5 Continue to shape the hollow until it is large enough to accommodate your hand when you grip the handle.

6 When the lid has dried to leather hard, trim it so that it fits snugly into the neck of the casserole. Redefine the ledge by neatening it with a trimming tool held against the side of it at an angle of 90°.

7 Carefully trim the centre of the lid to define the shallow central dome and ensure a good fit. Smooth over the trimmed form with a sponge.

Making the handle

1 If you decided to make the lid with the sunken centre, you will need to attach a handle. Extrude or pull a handle to a suitable length and leave it to stiffen.

2 Score the lid at opposite points on the ridge surrounding the central dip. Apply slurry and press the scored ends of the handle into place, ensuring a generous arch across the lid. Reinforce the joins with loops of clay pressed under the handle ends. △

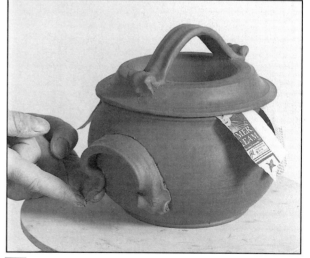

2 Press the lugs very firmly on to the wall of the casserole to ensure that they are bonded to the clay surface. If necessary reinforce the joins with small coils of clay. Smooth the joins with a damp sponge to seal them.

Attaching the lugs

1 Throw a low, baseless ring from 0.5kg (1lb) of clay. Slice this ring in half to form the two equal-sized lugs. Attach these lugs to the side of the casserole, first marking their position on the clay before scoring the surfaces to be joined and applying slurry.

Style B

1 Centre 1.5kg (3lbs) and throw a sturdy rounded pot in the same way as described for Casserole A, keeping a slightly thickened rim.

2 Raise the rim very slightly at the point on the circumference where you want to form the pouring lip. Form a pouring channel from the base upwards and ease the lip of this channel outwards. ◁

3 When the casserole has dried to leather hard, trim its base. Any vessel with a lip has to be cushioned with a clay coil when it is inverted. Measure the circumference of the casserole and draw a circle of the same size on the wheelhead. Make a thick clay coil to fit the circle. △

4 Flatten and trim the ring of clay and cut out a section so that there is no pressure on the lip of the inverted casserole. Turn the base as usual. If you want to fit a lid, make one in the same way as you did for Casserole A. ▷

Making the handle

1 Throw a hollow handle for this pouring casserole. Centre 0.5kg (1lb) of clay and raise it into a narrow pillar. Plumb down through the centre to the wheelhead and raise the cylinder, keeping a flared base. ◁

2 Gradually close the walls in with successive lifts, but do not close the handle over entirely; there should be a hole at its end. ▷

3 Shape the handle so that it is comfortable to grip, remembering that oven gloves will probably be worn when lifting the casserole. Use a throwing rib to compress the clay. Trim any waste clay from the base.

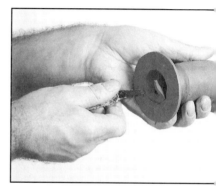

4 Once it has dried to leather hard, trim away any unwanted thickness from the inner edge and the base of the handle using a sharp knife.

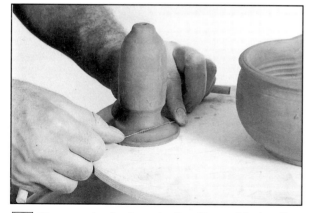

5 Slice away the clay from the flared base of the handle at a slight angle so that it will fit flush against the side of the casserole.

6 Score the area of the casserole where the handle is to go, apply slurry and press the handle in place. Smooth the flared base into the clay wall.

Casseroles

Functional ware used in connection with food must have
glazes that are easily cleaned. Although many clays are
"oven-proof" when fired, far fewer will withstand being
heated directly on a domestic cooker without cracking.

Dinner service

This project provides instructions for only the most basic components of a dinner service. You can adapt the tableware projects described elsewhere in the book to supplement the dinner plates and sauce boat and create a matching set.

1 For each plate, centre 2kg (4lbs) of clay. Spread the clay across the wheelhead and using the outside edge of your palm, open the clay into a very shallow plate. Keep the clay wet and use your fingers to continue shaping the plate. △

2 The plates will shrink when they are fired, so throw them to a wider diameter than that you actually require. Slightly compress the rim to give the plate a good firm edge.

3 Use a rib to smooth out the surface of the plate. Trim any excess clay away from the base, but do not take off too much because the edge of the plate might droop. Release the plate from the surface of the wheelhead with a wire.

4 When the plates are leather hard you can trim them. Invert a plate on the wheel and secure it with clay pellets. Turn the base, remembering that the plate is not particularly thick and not to pare away too much. Trim the outer edge. The larger plates will need a double footring, like the hors d'oeuvres tray (see p55). △

Making a serving plate

1 Make a large plate in the usual way. When it has dried to leather hard, slice two shallow eliptical shapes from opposite sides of the rim, leaving enough of the rim intact to prevent food sliding off the server. Smooth the shape off with a damp sponge. ◁

Making the sauce boat

1 Centre 0.6kg (1¼lbs) of well-prepared clay and throw a small, deep bowl. Collar the edge of it slightly to give it a full shape.

2 Gently compress the rim of the form to give it to strengthen it. Flare the edge slightly. Trim away any excess clay from the base and mop out any water.

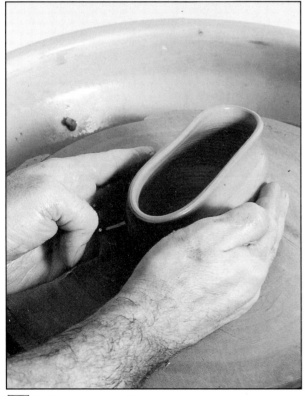

4 Form a generous pouring lip on its rim, by squeezing the rim at one end of the form very gently with your thumb and finger and easing out the clay between them. Leave the boat to dry to leather hard.

3 While the form is still soft, you can squash it gently into the traditional ovaled sauce boat shape, leaving the base circular. Take care not to close in the lips of the form too far.

Finishing touches

1 Invert and re-centre the sauce boat on the wheel, using the base area to guide you. Secure it with clay pellets. Turn the base carefully and give the form a narrow footring. ◁

2 Turn the sauce boat the right way up and with a suitable tool, mark two curved areas on either side of the rim. Cut these out with a sharp knife. These shallow dips on either side of the form accentuate its boat shape. Smooth the form off and tidy the rim. ▽

4 Invert the form on a suitable flat surface, allowing the loop of the handle to hang down while it dries so that it does not become distorted.

3 Extrude or pull a suitable handle for the sauce boat. Score the side of the rim at the back of the form and attach the handle firmly in a generous loop. Add a small coil of clay to strengthen the upper join.

Dinner set

Ilmenite oxide has been used to paint decorative bands on to the surface of the opaque white gloss. The speckling has been achieved by further spraying over the glazed surface, using an old toothbrush dipped in the oxide.

Coffee set

Both styles of coffee pot described in this project are based on a jug shape with an integral or a separately thrown spout. The proportions and design of the pot you throw should be echoed by the matching mugs, jug and sugar bowl.

Style A

1 Centre 2.2kg (4½lbs) of clay and draw it up into a tapered dome. Begin to lift the walls, maintaining a good width at the base of the form. Taper the walls gradually as you raise them, keeping a thick layer of clay around the rim from which to form the internal gallery.

2 Collar the neck of the form and define the point where it emerges from the body of the form. Remove any water before you close it in too far. Trim the rim and compress it. ▷

3 Split the rim with your thumb or fingernail to make an internal gallery. Trim around the inner edge of the ledge you have made. Measure the inner diameter of the throat of the jug so that you know how large to make the lid. △

4 Trim off any excess clay. When the pot has dried to leather hard, invert it on the wheelhead. Secure it with clay pellets and turn its base. ▷

Attaching a spout

1 Throw and attach a spout in the same way as you did for the teapots (*see p61*). You can either pierce a number of pouring holes in the wall of the pot, or one large one.

2 If you opt for the latter, bevel the lower inner edge to assist the flow of liquid. The unbevelled upper edge will stop the overflow of liquid as you pour.

Making the lid

1 Centre 170g (6oz) of clay and open it out, retaining a thick outer edge. Measure the diameter before you begin to make the flange. Split the rim with your thumb nail and depress the outer side to the wheelhead to form the flange. Raise the walls of the inner section. Trim the edge of the shape with a needle. Any final shaping can be done when the clay has dried further.

2 Shape a slight spout in the inner wall so that the lid sits snugly in the neck of the pot. When the lid is leather hard, trim it to a rounded dome and define a circle at the apex of the dome. Score this area and apply slurry. Attach a small lump of clay and with the minimum of water, throw a suitable knob.

Attaching the handle

Score the areas of the coffee pot's wall where the handle is to fit. Extrude or pull a handle of a suitable length and attach it with slurry having scored its ends. Add small clay coils to both joins to reinforce them. △

Style B

1 Centre 2.7kg (5½lbs) of clay and throw a similar shaped jug to that described above. Collar the top section slightly more vigorously, but keep plenty of clay around the rim. Flare the rim slightly.

2 Trim the rim and the upper section of the jug, leaving a bulge in the neck from which to spring a handle. Remove any water from within the form.

3 Smooth the rim with a sponge and flatten and compress it. Form an internal gallery, supporting the outside of the shape. Trim any excess clay from the base. Raise an area of the rim from which to form the pouring lip.

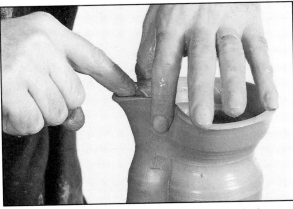

4 Smooth the edge of the internal gallery into the lip area. Using a long throwing rib, tease out the front section of the jug to form a long pouring channel. Shape the edge of the pouring lip with your fingers. △

5 Squeeze the neck of the jug to form an inner circle for the lid to sit in. When the pot has dried to leather hard, turn its base, cushioning its rim on a coil of clay to protect its spout. ▷

Attaching a handle

Make an identical lid to that described for style A, *(p86)* and attach an identical handle. Add a small piece of clay to the top of the handle and work it into the clay. Extend this to add a decorative flourish to the handle.

Decorating the pot

Decorate the body of the pot by incising lines into its surface. These cut lines produce very interesting effects when the pot is glazed. Invert the pot so that the handle hangs down as it dries.

Making the mugs

1 The mugs should all reflect the shape of the coffee pot. For each mug, centre 0.6kg (1¼lbs) of clay and throw a tapered cylinder with a flared rim.

2 Create a bulge in the wall of the mug at a point about a third of the way down. A handle will be attached at this point. Remove any water from the form and trim the base.

3 When the mug has dried to leather hard, invert it on the wheelhead and turn the base. Attach a handle that reflects the shape and design of the coffee pot's handle.

Making the jug

1 Centre 0.7kg (1½lbs) of clay and throw a shape similar to that described in making the mugs, but slightly larger. Leave a thickened rim from which to make the pouring lip.

2 Raise a small section of the rim and form a spout. Indent a pouring channel inside the jug and squeeze the lip area with your fingers. When it is leather hard, invert the jug, on a coil of clay, and turn its base.

3 Attach the handle in the same way as you attached the mug's. Again, it is important from the point of view of making a set that the curve and decorative design of the handle is similar for all the components.

Making the sugar bowl

1 Centre 0.6kg (1¼lbs) of clay and spread it into a shallow domed shape. Open the clay but still maintain the same basic shape and keep the raising of the wall to an absolute minimum.

2 Gently flare the rim and form a ridge at a point a third of the way down the wall. The bowl does not need a handle but this feature makes the bowl part of the set. Remove any water from inside the form and trim its base.

3 When the bowl has dried to leather hard, invert it on the wheelhead. Secure it with clay pellets and carefully turn its base.

Coffee set

Careful glazing of any set will help to unify all its different
components. Although a semi-matt oatmeal glaze was used
on these pieces, a shiny glaze has been used on the rims of
the mugs so that they are pleasant to drink from.

Carafe and goblet sets

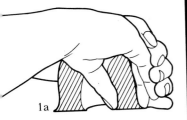

1a

Goblet A

1 Centre 0.7kg (1½lbs) of clay and form a narrow cone shape. Push your thumb through the clay right down to the wheelhead and draw the clay up in a hollow column.

Throwing a goblet will always present the potter with the problem of maintaining stability. Leaving aside the method whereby the cup and the stem are made separately and then joined together when leather hard, the two methods described here provide a logical solution to the problem of persuading a narrow stem of clay to support a larger cup.

2 Begin to create a conical shape, collaring after each lift. Swell a cup shape and sit back from the wheel to check its proportions. Shape the walls further and refine the rim. Collar the stem just below the swell of the cup. ▷

3 Continue to refine the shape of the goblet by throwing, and by trimming away the wet clay around the stem. When the goblet has dried to leather hard, trim the inner and outer edges of the base ring so that it will sit steadily.

4 To seal the goblet, cut out a small circle from a piece of flattened clay and attach it inside the goblet at the point where the swell of the cup joins the stem. Score the areas to be joined and apply slurry. Smooth the join over.

Goblet B

1 To make this style of goblet, centre the clay and draw up a narrow cone. Lifting your hands away from the wheelhead, apply pressure at a point 2cm (³⁄₄in) above the base. Keep the wheel rotating at an even speed. △

2 Continue to narrow the column until it is about 8.75cm (3½in) high. Begin to flare out a cup shape in the upper section by inserting your thumb to a depth of about 3.75cm (1½in).

3 Open and raise this section, ensuring that the cup you form has a good solid column of clay to support it. Check the evenness of the cup's curve by leaning back away from the wheel. Refine it as you wish.

4 Mop out any water from inside the cup. Raise the cup by collaring the stem of the goblet to thin it down. If you wish, you can develop a knuckle midway up the stem, (*see "Making a set" p33*). ◁

5 As the stem narrows, support the cup with your left hand. Further shaping can then take place without upsetting the balance of the goblet. Trim away any excess clay and shape the base of the goblet with a trimming tool.

The principle behind making any set is to maintain a unity of design through each component. These carafes are designed to echo the different styles of the goblets described in this project.

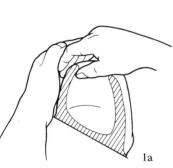

1a

Style A

1 Begin with 2.5kg (5lbs) of clay centred and flared out at the base. As you begin to raise the clay, maintain the lines of the initial conical profile by tapering as you lift.

2 As the form grows, define the point where the neck will emerge by collaring gently.

3a

3 Keep the upper cylindrical section relatively wide as you finish the lower half of the carafe. Mop out any water inside the form with a sponge.

4 Begin to collar the upper section fairly vigorously bearing in mind that you are aiming to form a narrow neck. Keep your eye on the point where the neck section begins.

6 Even off the walls of the base section with a throwing rib, supporting the neck as you go. Shape area where the swell of the base narrows into the neck.

5 As the upper portion narrows down, the walls will thicken providing you with plenty of clay from which to throw the neck of the form. Lift the narrowed shape smoothly and evenly and keep the whole form steadied.

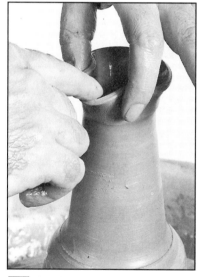

8 Thin the rim at one point with your thumb and forefinger to increase the workable area from which to create a spout. Hold the edge of this area of the rim with two fingers and tease out a spout.

7 Taper the neck of the carafe and begin to open the rim out to form a flared edge. Tidy off any ragged edges around the rim. When the carafe has dried to leather hard, you can attach a handle if you wish (see "Handles", p29).

Style B

1 Centre 2.5kg (5lbs) of clay. Draw the clay in at the base, rather than flaring it out. This establishes the basic form of the carafe. From the very first lift, you should try to encourage the development of a spherical base section by pulling up, and simultaneously pushing outwards.

2 Begin to collar the shape bringing the clay up from the base. Mop out any water. Keep the base steady and begin to close in the upper portion of the form, narrowing the neck while still maintaining the swell of the base. ◁

3 Compressing a ridge at the point where the neck emerges from the base will help to prevent the base sagging as you work on the upper section, lifting and tapering the neck. Trim the rim off with a pin and smooth it down with a sponge.

4 Define the lip of the carafe using a rib and pass the rib down the neck to even and smooth the clay surface. Trim away any excess clay at the base. If you wish you can attach a slender handle once the carafe has dried to leather hard (*see "Handles", p29*).

5 Thin the rim at one point with your thumb and forefinger to form the area from which to make a spout. Hold the edge of the rim with two fingers and ease out a spout.

Carafes and goblets

A simple brushed design can be achieved with loosely
applied brushstrokes to produce an attractive, informal set.
If you are worried that your design might look untidy, brush
it on a glaze that will run and blur during firing.

Lamp base

The technique involved in this project is that of constructing a large composite form. It can of course be adapted to make any form that you feel is too large for you to throw as one piece. An interesting decorative motif, such as the one illustrated, will add a new perspective to this lamp base and make it a unique and personal possession.

2 Define the shape of the cylinder and compress its walls with a trimming tool or rib. Trim the rim with a needle and compress it. Remove any water from the form.

1 Centre 2.5kg (5lbs) of clay. The lamp will be more stable if its base is broader than its upper section, so bear this in mind as you start to throw. Raise and taper the walls gently with successive lifts.

4 Decorate the base of the form with clay roulettes. You can make these by impressing a texture into discs of plastic clay and then biscuit-firing them. They have holes in their centres through which a piece of wire is threaded so that these "wheels" can be rolled over the surface of a pot to produce a decorative imprint. It is best to leave the clay form until it has stiffened before decorating it, because the impressed pattern will show up more clearly.

3 With calipers measure the outer diameter of the rim. This measurement is crucially important because it will dictate the width of the upper section of the lamp base.

Making the upper section

1 Centre 2.5kg (5kg) of clay and open it out to the correct diameter, right down to the wheelhead. The shape of the cylinder you throw is a matter of personal preference – you can extend it as a straight form or develop a swell in the walls.

2 To give the form a swell at its base, ease the clay out smoothly from a point about 1cm ($^2/_5$in) above the level of the wheelhead, ensuring that you do not alter the width. ▷

3 Whichever method you choose, collar the upper section of the cylinder to form a neck into which a bulb fitting can be inserted. Smooth off the rim with a sponge and trim away any excess clay from the base.

4 Check the outer base diameter using calipers and adjust it using a trimming tool if it is too wide to fit on to the neck of the lower section.

5 You can either leave the top section of the lamp plain, or decorate it to match the lower section. An interesting way to echo the design would be to decorate the clay within a band area outlined around the form.

6 Join the two sections when they have stiffened. Score the top rim of the lower section and the adjoining rim of the upper. Apply slurry to the edge of the lower section and press the pieces together. Smooth and seal the join. Running a decorated clay roulette around the join will disguise it very well. ◁

7 Using a piercing tool, gently make a hole in the wall of the lamp base at a point near its base. This allows the electric cable to be attached. If the opening at the top of the lamp base is too large for a standard light fitting, you can fit a wide cork inside it, cut specifically to hold the fitting. △

Lamp base

Iron oxide was rubbed into the richly textured surface of the lamp base to colour it without obscuring the relief. The top section was then dipped in an opaque white glaze. The iron oxide altered the colour of the glaze.

Candle holders

The essence of any candle holder is the siting of the candle, and its capacity to contain the molten wax. The first of these candle holders is made to a traditional portable design, while the second is more like a night light. Both involve the same technique.

Style A

1 Centre 1.2kg (2½lbs) of clay into a low dome. Begin to open the clay using both your forefingers, pressing into the dome at a point, about 2.5cm (1in) from its centre. This causes a solid pillar of clay to emerge in the exact centre of the form. ▷

2 Raise the outer walls with one finger, forming a trough-like collar around the central pillar of clay. Shape the rim of this collar by compressing it and gently easing the outer edge of it over your fingers. △

3 Hollow out the clay pillar by plumbing into it with your finger. Shape the wall to match the thickness of the outer wall. Once the basic candle siting has emerged, you can modify its height and design. It is a good idea to extend the candle holder above the level of the outer wall.

5 Score the flattened area of the form. Score the end of the handle, apply slurry and press it into place. Ensure that the loop of the handle provides a comfortable grip. Invert the candle holder so that the handle loop does not droop during drying.

4 Remove any water from the shape and trim any excess clay away from the base. Gently flatten one side of the circular form to create a surface on which to attach a widely looped handle. Leave the form to dry to leather hard.

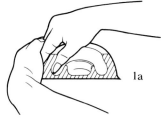

1a

Style B

1 Centre 2.5kg (3lbs) of clay and raise it into a high, narrow dome. Push down through the clay at the apex of the dome with your thumb, to a depth of about 2.5cm (1in).

2 Continue to exert pressure, but push out at an angle towards the outer edge of the base, thus forming a central peak within the wide cone shape. Once the peak is formed, impress your finger into its top, forming an open cuff in which to stand a candle.

3 Begin to raise the outer walls around the central candle siting, drawing the mass of clay up from the base. Collar the walls slightly as you lift them to maintain a beehive shape.

4 Collar the clay quite firmly to emphasize the swell of the walls above the candle cuff and increase the thickness of clay around the rim from which to extend the form.

5 Finalize the lifting of the outer wall and begin to close the rim inwards to form a narrowed lip. Trim off the rim of the form with a needle.

6 Add definition and strength to the walls of the shape by compressing it with a throwing rib. Impress a slight ledge into the upper section so that the ultimate shape of the candle holder resembles a night light. Trim away any excess clay from the base.

7 When the form has dried to leather hard, mark the area you will cut out on the side of it. Any shape is perfectly acceptable – the hole simply has to be large enough to allow the candle light to shine out.

8 Using a pin, cut through the wall of the form following the guideline of the shape you have drawn and remove the segment of clay. Be careful not to cut out your shape at a point too near the base, where the clay is thick. Tidy off the edges of the hole and smooth the shape with a sponge.

Candle holders

A basic matt white glaze was used on both these candle
holders. A second darker glaze was then poured over to
break up the overall pale colour and give the shapes a
further dimension.

Potpourri

Literally translated, "pot pourri" means rotten pot which graphically describes the appearance of this pierced pot. The fragrances of the dried flowers and scented herbs with which it is filled permeate the atmosphere via these holes. This particular design allows the pot to be hung or free-standing.

Making the base

1 Centre 2kg (4lbs) of clay and draw it up into a rounded shape. As you raise the walls, ensure that there is plenty of clay around the rim from which to make the internal ledge. ◁

2 Spread the thickness of clay at the rim over the top of your left forefinger, held within the pot. The clay at the rim of the pot will flatten and extend inwards to form a smooth ledge. △

3 Smooth off and compress the outside of the pot with a rib and tidy the rim. Trim away any excess clay from the edge of the ledge with a needle and remove any water from within the form. △

4 Measure the outer diameter of the rim with a pair of calipers so that you know how wide to make the top.

Making the top

1 Centre 1.2kg (2½lbs) of well-prepared clay and form it into a shallow dome. Open it out down to the wheelhead to the correct diameter, pushing outwards with your thumb. △

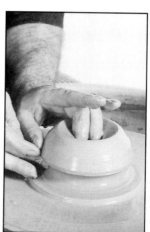

2 Lift the wall, forming the two ledges immediately. Collar the clay briefly just above the base. Allow the clay to open and then close in above this second ridge. ◁

4 Flatten the upper spout into a fan shape. Slice through the base with a cutting wire to release the clay from the wheelhead. △

3 Swell the walls of the form to give a good rounded shape. Close in the top section, finishing the edge off into a short neck. Trim the top and the base of the form. △

5 When the lid has dried to leather hard, invert it in a suitable chuck on the wheelhead and trim its underside. Trim the lower ledge to correspond with the main body width. ▷

The finishing touches

1 When the base has dried to leather hard, invert and centre it on the wheelhead. If you want to hang the pot, you can trim the base completely round; if you want to keep your options open, trim the base flat so that you can stand or hang it. Trim the two pieces so that they share the same outer diameter.

2 Cut out two sections from the rim of the bottom half, using guidelines measured with a ruler.

4 With a piercing tool, make several holes in the bottom half, creating as simple or as elaborate a design as you wish. If you want to suspend the pot, pierce a hole in the top of the lid.

3 Cut out two sections from the upper half, creating ledges that are the same size as the cut-out areas of the bottom half. Use the same measurement guidelines to do this. Trim these projecting ledges so that they slot easily into the gaps in the lower rim.

Pot pourri

The many decorative holes of the pot have been highlighted with cobalt oxide. The oxide was brushed over a matt white glaze to produce this soft blue colour. The colours of the pot pourri petals add to the decorative scheme of the form.

Mirror frame

A mirror or indeed a picture frame can be made with equal ease by following this simple method. The frame need not be circular: it can be shaped into an oval or a square. If you do change the shape of the form, you should trim it while it is pliable.

1 Centre about 1kg (2lbs) of clay and flatten it into a shallow dome. With your thumb, push down through the clay to the wheelhead. Open the clay out by pushing with both thumbs in opposite directions. As you widen the ring of clay, press down on to the surface of the clay with the base of your thumbs to prevent it splitting.

2 Indent the surface of the ring with your finger. Smooth the form over and trim its inner and outer edges. There are many different ways of decorating the frame. You could apply a light-coloured slip and draw on a darker design with a slip trailer.

3 You could roll a long coil of clay and make a pattern by pressing it into the indent of the frame. Clay pellets can also be added. You could use different colour clays, or different coloured slips. A clay roulette could be used to impress a pattern into the surface of the frame. Use a roller to flatten the pattern you have chosen to create.

4 When the frame has dried to leather hard, invert it on the wheelhead and secure it with clay pellets. Trim away any ragged edges and form an inner ledge, deep enough for the mirror or the picture, backing card and glass.

5 To hang the frame, pierce a hole at a suitable point on the perimeter of the frame, or attach a coil of clay in a small loop.

Mirror or picture frame

Iron oxide was brushed onto the surface of the frame and
then wiped off the raised surface. A shiny glaze was brushed
over its inner and outer edges to produce further textural
contrasts.

Self-draining plant pot

Most people have their own favourite houseplants and like to keep them in attractive containers. This self-draining plant pot combines good looks with utility. It is sturdy, well-balanced and its drainage holes enable you to plant directly into it.

1 Centre 2kg (4lbs) of well-prepared clay and form it into a full dome. Once the clay is centred, move your hands so that you are applying pressure at a point 1.8cm (³⁄₄in) above the level of the wheelhead.

2 As pressure is applied a thick basal collar of clay will emerge – this will be used to form the drainage tray. Supporting the clay with your palms, begin to plumb into the dome with your thumbs.

3 Open out the main body of clay, steering clear of the clay collar at its base. Gradually lift the wall, shaping it so that it flares gently outwards with successive lifts.

4 Refine the edge of the rim with your fingertips, easing it up and out over the fingers of your supporting hand. Link up your hands for extra support. △

5 Finalize the shaping of the pot's rim by pushing the clay out against a rubber kidney and simultaneously indenting the body of the pot just below the rim. ▷

6 To make the drainage tray, impress the clay collar at the base of the pot using your right forefinger. Support your right hand with your left and ensure that you keep the pressure exerted by keeping your forefinger steady. △

7 Extend the wall to a suitable height, shaping its edge with your fingers to reflect the shape of the rim of the pot. Be careful not to distort the walls of the pot. ▷

8 Any refining of the shape of the drainage tray can be undertaken when you trim the base of the form to remove excess clay. Hold the trimming tool steadily against the side of the tray's wall as you pare the clay away.

9 Remove any water from inside the pot and the drainage tray using a small sponge. Smooth down the rim with a damp sponge or a strip of chamois leather.

Finishing touches

1 Once the pot has dried to leather hard, turn its base. Because of the raised internal pot shape, the base is relatively thick and quite a large amount of clay can be pared away. △

2 Using a piercing tool, make four drainage holes at the base of the pot. Hold the tool at an angle to the wall of the pot to ensure that the holes made allow water to drain away easily. ◁

Self-draining plant pot

Glazes of a fairly neutral colour are the best choice for
decorating a plant pot, so that there is no risk of the pot
detracting from the beauty of the species of plant it
contains.

Puzzle jug

The puzzle jug is a traditional vessel that has re-emerged recently as a popular novelty. Puzzle jugs are traditionally associated with bucolic celebrations, where they provided party-goers with an amusing test of skill. Nowadays, that same test has lost none of its appeal; nor has the attractive design of the jug.

1a
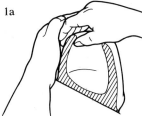

1 Centre 1.5kg (3lbs) of well-prepared clay. Throw a basic jug shape, swelling the clay out to form a belly and collaring for a neck. As you lift the walls of the form, keep in mind the shape you are aiming for.△

2 When you reach the rim, keep the clay fairly thick as you will need plenty of scope to successfully create the special puzzle rim. Trim the rim with a needle and begin to form the looped rim.

3 Flare out the rim until it is almost flat, supporting its underside with your left forefinger. Continue to maintain this support and start to exert pressure downwards with your right forefinger so that the clay begins to curl round towards the neck of the jug. △

4 When the rim has curved round to meet the wall of the jug, seal the join with a modelling tool. Take out any water and trim around the base. ▷

Making the handle

1 The handle is made by cutting a suitable length from a hollow ring of clay. Centre 0.5kg (1lb) of clay. Push your thumb down through the clay to meet the surface of the wheelhead and open it out as you would if you were making a shallow dish.

3 Before you close the form completely, make a hole in the inner wall to allow the escape of any air. Seal the ring with a trimming tool. Remove any clay around the inner and outer edges of the ring with a trimming tool to give it a smooth, rounded shape. Leave the ring to stiffen before cutting a handle. ▽

2 Open out the form to create a slim ring of clay. Support the sides of the ring with your left hand and using your right forefinger, impress a ridge into the clay. The ring will gradually divide and a shallow cuff will emerge. Neaten the edges of the cuff with your fingertips. Start to extend the outer wall gently, encouraging the clay to curve towards the inner wall. When the clay walls have met, use your fingers to seal the two edges together.

Making the spouts

1 Throw the spouts using a technique known as "stack-throwing", where several small forms are thrown from the top of a clay stack. Centre a good-sized lump of clay, and lift it into a cone. Push your fingertip down into the clay to a depth that corresponds to the height of the spouts. Shape this indented section into a thick-lipped spout.

2 Cut off the spout section using a needle. The segment you remove from the clay should be completely hollow. Throw several spouts of the same general size.

The finishing touches

1 Turn the base of the jug when it is leather hard. Using a piercing tool, make several holes around the neck section of the jug. The pattern of holes can be as simple or elaborate as you wish. Smooth the edges when dry.

2 Shape a section of the handle to fit the jug. Pierce one hole in the jug at a point 2–3cm (³/₄–1¹/₄in) up from the base, another in the rim directly above this hole, and a third in the upper curve of the handle itself. Blow down the handle to check that it is not blocked. Score around the two holes in the jug and the cut surfaces of the handle. Attach the handle to the jug with slurry, ensuring that the holes in the rim and at the base of the jug are lined up with the hollow handle. Smooth the joins over, supporting the jug with your other hand.

4 Attach all the other spouts you have made in the same way, but without making a hole in the rim of the jug. Paint the body of the jug with a coloured slip so that you can scratch a traditional puzzle jug verse on to the jug's surface when the slip dries.

3 Make a genuine hole for a spout in the rim of the jug opposite the handle. Flatten the base of the spout out a little. Score the surface of the rim around the spout hole, and the flattened surface of the spout. Attach the spout to the rim with slurry, being careful not to clog the hole. △

5 This is a process known as "sgraffito". The contrasting colour of the clay beneath the slip brings a touch of life to the jug, and you can choose the words you want to inscribe to suit any special occasion. Traditional verses, however, do seem to be more appropriate.

Puzzle jugs

Here are two traditional verses to inscribe on puzzle jugs. A simple transparent glaze has been used to ensure that the verses remain legible.

Here gentlemen come try your skill.
I'll hold a wager if you will
That you can't drink this liqor all.
Without you spill or let some fall.

Within this jug there be good liqor,
Fit for parson or for vicar.
But to drink and not to spill
Will try the utmost of your skill.

Bird and animal forms

A ll these little creatures are thrown following a very similar basic technique which readily adapts itself to produce a variety of very different shapes. There is plenty of scope for inventing your own favourites, developing your own additions from these initial ideas and incorporating your own decorative innovations.

Gull

1 Centre 0.8kg (1¾lbs) of clay. Throw a narrow cone and as it grows collar the form in. Continue to lift the walls swelling the base of the cylinder out slightly. Take out any water from inside the shape with a sponge.

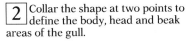

2 Collar the shape at two points to define the body, head and beak areas of the gull.

3 Taper and close the final beak section until it takes the form of a fine, elongated cone. Trim off any unevenness at its end. △

4 When the form is closed, you can modify the shape of the gull's head and body — the middle and lower sections of the form. Collar the head section until it is in proportion with the rest of the form. Trim away any excess clay from the base.

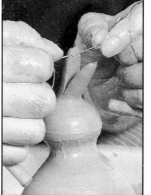

6 Stop the wheel and continue to alter the angle that the head and beak make with the gull's body. Split the beak section carefully with a taut wire and ease the two flaps this creates slightly apart to give the gull an open beak.◁

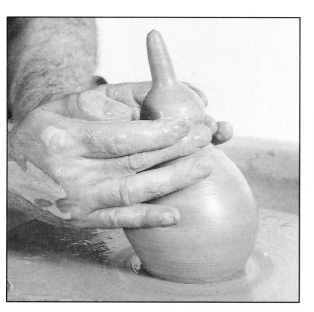

5 To give the gull a more realistic attitude, carefully shift its head section slightly off centre so that it points away from the form at a gentle angle. Lubricate the clay generously as you mould the angle.◁

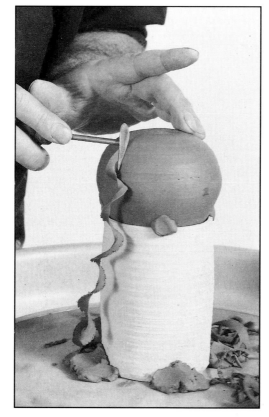

7 Use a thrown cylinder or a suitable piece of tubing for the chuck to trim the base of the gull once it is leather hard. Invert the gull into the chuck and secure it with small pellets of clay. Trim its base until it has a smooth rounded shape, then push the gull down on to a flat surface at an angle. Tap it gently until it has a steady resting base. Pierce a hole in the base to release the air pressure.

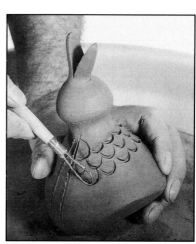

8 Add decorative "bird-like" features to the gull using a looped wire tool. Define the wing area and the plummage. Once the decoration is defined, cut into the clay to give the features some depth. Draw on the eyes with the looped wire.

Owl

1 Centre 0.8kg (1¾lbs) of clay. Throw a narrow cylinder and begin to taper it slightly. Swell the lower section of the form, but begin to narrow it at a point about two thirds of the way up the form so as to create an upper section for the owl's head.

2 Begin to collar this upper section, but ensure that you leave a large enough gap to be able to use one finger to continue to raise the form and shape the head.

3 When you are happy with the proportions of the owl, take out any water with a sponge on a stick and close the shape over. Trim away any excess clay from around the base.

4 Modify the shape further if you wish once the form is closed. Define the eye areas on the head section by pressing and rubbing gently with your fingers. Leave the shape to dry to leather hard.

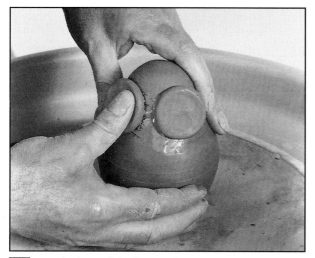

6 Impress the plummage on the owl's breast with a looped wire tool. Cut into these markings to give them an interesting texture. Brush off any excess clay.

5 Trim the base of the form in the same way you did the gull. Stand the owl upright. Make two small discs of clay from two clay balls. Score the eye areas and attack the discs with slurry. Make concentric imprints in the discs using any appropriate round object, completing the eyes with a central circle. △

7 Define the wing areas on the sides of the owl. Holding the owl firmly but carefully, score decorative feather markings down over the clay with a suitable tool.◁

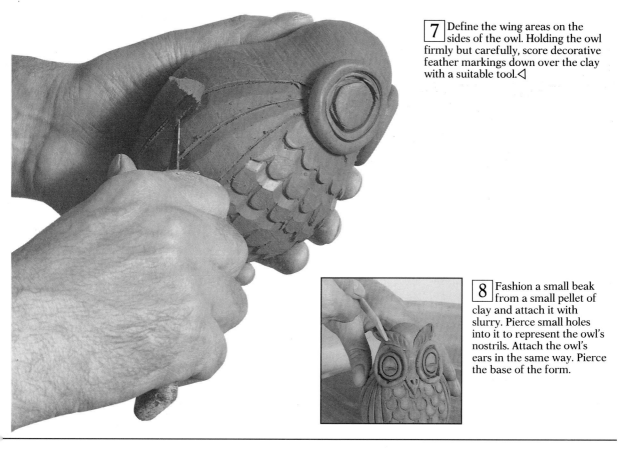

8 Fashion a small beak from a small pellet of clay and attach it with slurry. Pierce small holes into it to represent the owl's nostrils. Attach the owl's ears in the same way. Pierce the base of the form.

Hedgehog

1 Centre 0.8kg (1¾lbs) of clay and draw it into a squat dome shape. Begin to open the shape, aiming for a rounded shape as you lift the walls.

2 Collar in quite tightly at a point about one third of the way down the shape, thereby forming a narrowed upper section. Take out any water with a sponge on a stick. ▽

3 Support the lower rounded shape as you continue to narrow the emerging neck into a thin cylindrical pipe — this will eventually be the hedgehogs snout. Trim off the rim of this pipe with a pin.

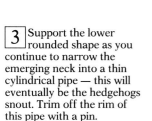

4 Continue to shape the snout, adding a knuckle if you want to. Trim away any excess clay from the base. To make the hedgehog look more realistic, move the snout slightly off centre until it points out at an angle. Leave the form to dry to leather hard. Trim the base of the hedgehog and flatten it so that the hedgehog sits at an angle.

5 Pierce two eye holes in the form just above the snout and finish the eyes by drawing eyebrows with a looped wire tool. To make the hedgehog's "spines", push a lump of clay through a sieve and cut off the extruded lengths. Apply slurry to the hedgehog's back and stick the clay spines either all over it, or on the top of the hedgehog's head. If you opt for the second method, score spine-like lines on the hedgehog's body. △

Bird and animal forms

Manganese dioxide has been used to accentuate the
"feathers" of the gull and the owl. Both a matt and an
opaque white glaze were used for these shapes. Leaving part
of a shape unglazed can be effective.

Chess set

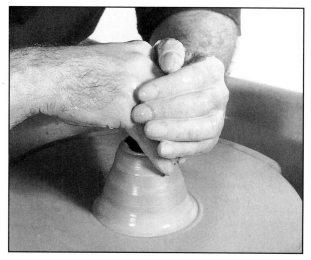

Throwing a chess set is a test of both imagination and creative skill. Choose your own decorative theme, remembering that as long as the different pieces are easily recognizable, they can all be individually characterized.

Making the pawns

1 For each pawn, centre 0.5kg (1lb) of clay. Form it into a narrow dome shape with the diameter you want the pieces to have. Plumb through the clay to the wheelhead and raise and taper the walls.

2 Roughly define the head and body areas with successive lifts. Begin to collar the shape at its rim and finally close it over entirely. Any further shaping can take place at this stage.

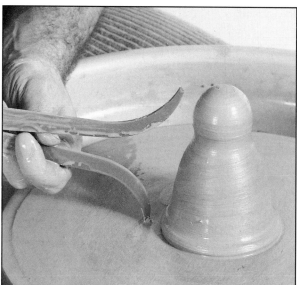

3 Form a small ledge around the base to help balance the shape. Trim away any excess clay and smooth the shape off. ◁

4 Measure the height and width of the form so that you have a constant sizing for all the pawns. △

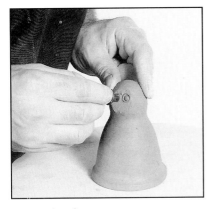

Decorating the pawns

1 When the pawns are leather hard, trim around their bases to give them a uniform silhouette. The way you characterize the pawns, or indeed any of the pieces, is of course up to you. As long as the pieces are recognizable you can decorate them exactly as you wish.

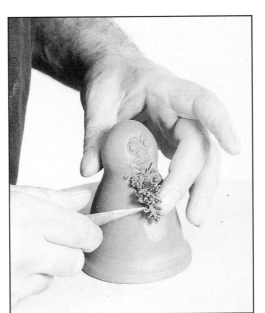

2 Slice a section off the front of the head to make a face. Paint this area with slurry and make the pawn's features by pressing small pellets of clay into place and marking the clay. Make a beard by forcing a lump of clay through a sieve to make shreds of clay, as you did for the hedgehog, *(see p124).*

3 Attach a coil of clay around the neck of the pawn and decorate it. The arms can be made by simply shaping two small pieces of clay and attaching them with slurry to meet across the belly. Model the hands from two small balls of clay.

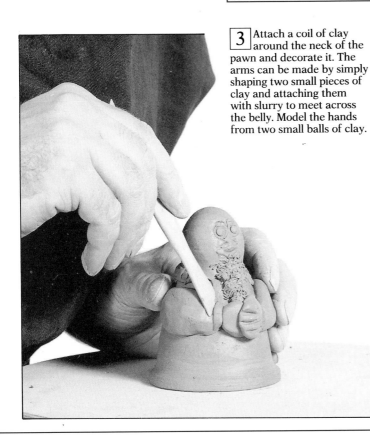

4 Indent a pattern around the base of the form with a suitable tool. Repeat the same decorative features on all the pawns to make a set.

Making the bishops and the knights

1 Both the bishop and the knight are basically the same shape and height. Centre 0.7kg (1½lbs) and throw a form following the directions described for the pawns, but make sure that it is noticeably taller.

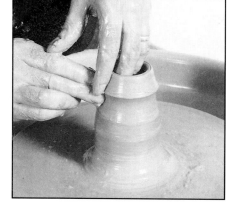

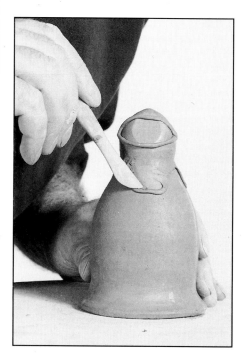

2 Define the difference between the two pieces when you form the head and body areas. Take out any water from within the form. Collar and close its top over and finalise any shaping. Indent a ledge at the base of the form and trim away any excess clay.

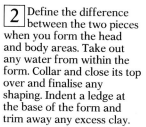

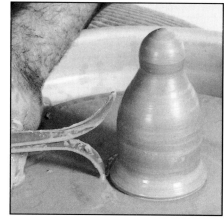

Decorating the knight

1 Define the knight's armour by attaching a thin coil of clay around the "shoulders" of the form. Make his visor by attaching an eliptical loop of clay coil across his head.

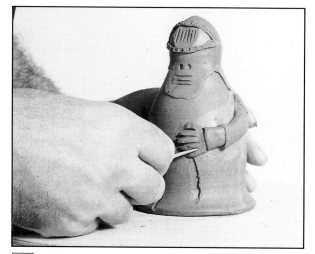

2 Model a pair of arms as you did for the pawn, and attach them with slurry. Place a clay coil around his wrists and model his hands.

3 Flatten a piece of clay and cut out a long shield shape. Attach a clay coil heraldic decoration to the shield with slurry. Press the shield in place on the Knight.

Decorating the bishop

1 Slice off a section of the head to make a face. Add the details of his face and a long beard. Flatten a piece of clay and cut out two mitre shapes. Join them together and attach the mitre to the top of the bishop's head with slurry. Press a clay coil around the edge of the mitre and indent a cross into the front of it.

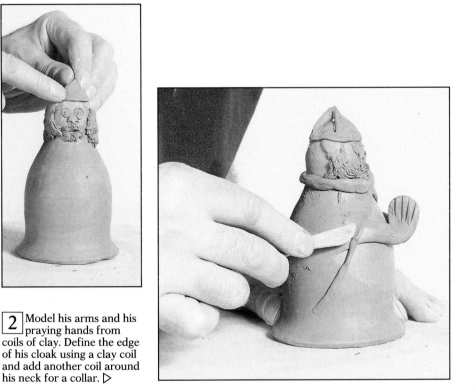

2 Model his arms and his praying hands from coils of clay. Define the edge of his cloak using a clay coil and add another coil around his neck for a collar. ▷

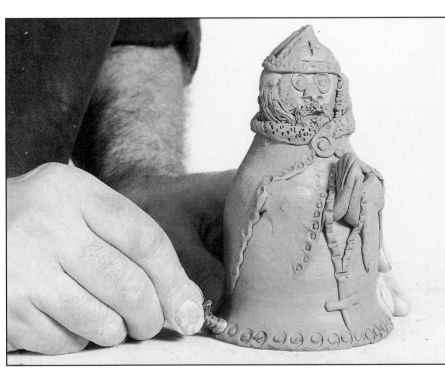

3 With a very fine coil of clay, make a rosary and attach it so that he seems to be clasping it in his hands. Decorate the edge of his cloak and gown with a suitable tool.

Making the castles

1 For each castle, centre 0.5kg (1lb) of clay and raise a straight sided cylinder. The castles should be taller than the pawns.

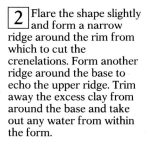

2 Flare the shape slightly and form a narrow ridge around the rim from which to cut the crenelations. Form another ridge around the base to echo the upper ridge. Trim away the excess clay from around the base and take out any water from within the form.

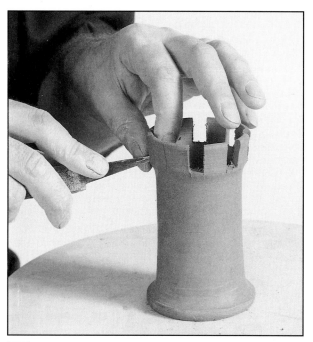

3 When the form is leather hard, turn the base if necessary. To make the crenelations, mark out the clay to be removed and carefully cut out the clay pieces, using a sharp knife. Smooth the edges down.

4 Decorate the walls of the castle with thin coils of clay, attached with slurry and smoothed into the body of the form, or left as a relief.

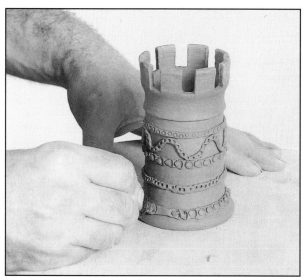

5 How you shape these coils is up to you. With a suitable implement you can apply textures and specific patterns to give the clay an interesting texture.

2 Define four body areas. Collar the cylinder in the areas corresponding to her waist, her neck and the top of her head. The uppermost section will be her crown, so ensure that it is evenly flared. Trim the edge of her crown and indent a ledge around the base. When the form is leather hard you can decorate it.

Making the queens

1 Both kings and queens are made in the same way, with the shaping of their bodies serving to distinguish between them. Centre 1kg (2lbs) of clay to make the queen. Throw a straight-sided cylinder that tapers towards its rim.

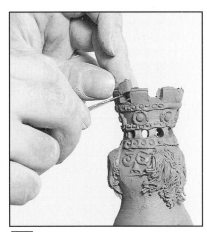

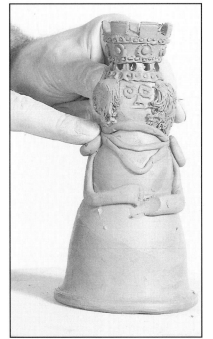

3 Define the crown area with a knife. Slice off a section of clay from the head area to form a face. Apply slurry to the face and attach clay pellets to make the Queen's eyes and nose. Define her eyebrows, eyes and mouth with a suitable tool. Push a lump of clay through a sieve to make her hair. Attach the hair just beneath her crown.

4 Decorate her crown in any way you think appropriate — piercing holes and adding coils and pellets of clay. Cut out an interesting design from the rim of the crown. Model a pair of arms from lengths of clay.

5 Use clay coils to define the shape and detail of her clothes. Model some shoulder ruffles and cuffs around her wrists. Fashion her hands from clay. Score and impress her "skirt" to give it the look of fabric.

Making the kings

1 Centre 1.1kg (2¼lbs). Extend the height of the cylinder beyond the height of the queen.

2 Instead of collaring three times to shape the piece only collar to define his head and his crown — the King has a portly silhouette.

3 Trim the edge of the crown carefully with a needle and indent a smooth decorative ledge around the base using a throwing rib

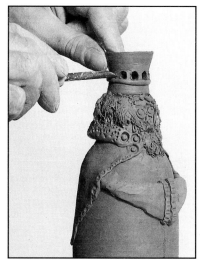

Decorating the kings

1 When the form is leather hard, define the crown area with a knife. Make the king's face and a majestic beard. Attach a thick coil of clay around the back of his neck to give the appearance of a fur collar.

2 Make some hair in the usual way and attach it beneath his crown. Attach two clay coils to the sides of his body for arms and flatten them into sleeves. Use another clay coil to define the edge of his cloak, leading from his neck down and around his back.

3 Add any surface patterns to the cloak with a suitable tool. Decorate the crown to give the impression of jewels and cut crenelations into its rim.

Chess set

A chess set does not have to be black and white, as long as
one set is glazed in a lighter colour than the other. The
surface quality of the chosen glaze is important, because a
high gloss may detract from the decoration of the pieces.

Fantasy castle

A castle is traditionally associated with mystery and suspense; its silhouette alone can sometimes be enough to conjure up a sense of impending romantic adventure. The success of this project relies on the creative arrangement of its component cylinders. If the castle is to be lit up from within, the greater the number of turrets, the greater the visual impact will be.

1 Centre 3.5kg (7lbs) of clay and throw a tall, tapering cylinder. The taller the cylinder is, the more impressive the end result will be. Compress the sides of the cylinder with a throwing rib to strengthen and shape the walls. Trim off any unevenness at the top of the cylinder.

2 Throw an identical second cylinder, and then a series of cylinders of varying sizes from which to make the turrets. Throw a squat, tapered cylinder with a base that measures twice the width of the first two cylinders. Leave them aside to stiffen. ▷

3 To make the roofs of the castle, stack-throw a series of varying conical forms. These cones will be stuck to the different cylinders at irregular angles to give the castle a romantic feel. Centre 0.3–0.7kg (¾–1½lbs) of clay and begin to raise a V-shaped cone. △

4 Trim it away at its base to emphasize its point and slice it from the stack of clay. Repeat this process until you have thrown several slightly different forms. Leave them at one side to stiffen slightly. ▽

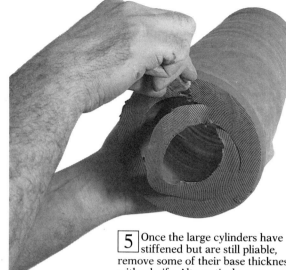

5 | Once the large cylinders have stiffened but are still pliable, remove some of their base thickness with a knife. Alternatively, you can turn the forms in the usual way. △

6 | With a sharp knife, slice vertically through one side of the walls of both cylinders. Open each cylinder out, easing the opening gradually wider. ▷

7 | Gently bend the walls inwards until the cylinders look like two curved "W"s. Stand the two opened shapes next to each other and level off any difference in height.

8 | Pare away the clay at an angle from the cut surfaces of the two forms, so that they fit together snugly when joined. Score the surfaces to be joined, apply slurry and press the pieces together. Smooth the joins firmly. Attach a coil of clay to the outside of each join and smooth it into place.

Assembling the pieces

1 Score the top of the castle base and apply slurry. Take the short tapered cylinder and carefully score its base. Join this cylinder to the top of the castle base. ▷

2 Smooth the cylinder into place over the castle, moulding the clay edges together to give the castle an overall rounded shape and seal the join. △

3 Centre a large roof cone and trim away the clay from its peak to make it rounded and more dome-like in shape. With a throwing rib, impress a cuff into the top of the roof for an additional decorative touch. △

4 Attach it to the castle having scored the adjacent surfaces and applied slurry. Be careful not to distort the shape of the roof as you fix it in place.

5 Cut out a side section from one of the small cylinders so that it will sit in against the side of the castle shape. Roughly mark out the area on the castle to which this small tower is to be attached and score the surface of the clay. Apply slurry and press the tower into place.

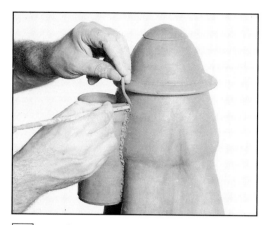

6 Smooth the join carefully, reinforcing it with a coil of clay. Press the coil into place neatly using a wooden tool. Smooth the form off with a damp sponge. △

7 Pinch the top of a small roof cone, similar in diameter to the little tower. Cut out a curve in its wall so that it will fit neatly against the side of the castle. Score the surfaces to be joined, apply slurry and press the roof into place. Arrange a series of these small towers around the walls of the castle at different heights. You can mould them in any way you wish while they are still wet to create the castle design you have in mind.

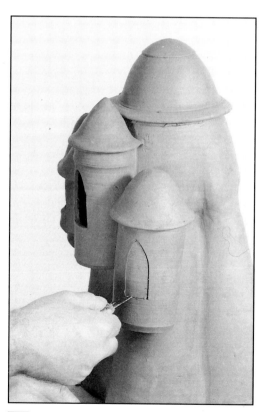

9 To decorate the roofs, roll out a sheet of clay and cut it up into little squares. Score the roofs, apply slurry and attach rows of these squares to give the effect of uneven tiles. Begin at the lower edge of the roof, smoothing the upper edge of each row before beginning the next. △

8 Cut out little windows in the walls of all the towers and corresponding holes in the wall of the castle behind these windows to allow the light through from within the castle. △

10 Leave the uppermost part of each roof bare and complete the layers of "tiles" with a thin coil of clay. Smooth this coil into the surface of the exposed roof. You can add as much detail as you want to the basic castle shape, adding more turrets until you feel happy with the silhouette you have created.

The finishing touches

1 To make the entrance to the castle, mark out an arched area midway up the side of the castle. Draw a zigzag line about a third of the way down from the upper curve and etch vertical lines down the top section to give the impression of a portcullis. Cut out the section of clay below the zigzag line with a knife and tidy the edge with a needle. Cut out several small blocks of flattened clay to make window ledges. Score them and attach them with slurry to the wall of the castle below each window. Smooth the join well.

2 To make the winding staircase leading from the portcullis entrance, cut out a slightly triangular piece of flattened clay. Score the side of it and attach it with slurry to the wall of the castle below the entrance. Press it round following the curve of the wall. Attach several flat blocks of clay beneath this main step, overlapping each one in an irregular fashion, both to provide support and give the impression of a romantically worn stairway. △

3 You can wind the staircase around the wall of the castle as far as you wish. Trim around the base with a sharp knife to improve the finish of the castle and smooth the whole shape off.

Fantasy castle

The castle was glazed with a matt white glaze and then
sprayed with iron oxide. The roof tiles were wiped clean and
brushed with iron oxide alone, for a contrast in both colour
and texture between the roof, the steps, and the walls.

Index

Acknowledgments

The author and publisher would like to thank the
following people and organizations for their kind help
in the production of this book:

Potterycrafts Ltd., Campbell Road, Stoke-on-Trent,
for their generosity in supplying the wheel, the tools
and the clay for use in the book, and especially Ken
Shelton, their Marketing Manager, for his assistance:
Mr. A.V. Evershed (Principal) and Mr. R.A. Clarke
(Head of Department) of Milton Keynes College:
Craftsmen Potters Association for the loan of the
tools for the front cover photograph; Bruton
Photography, 22, Bruton Street, London W1X 7DA.